31050002008108

D0984825

THE
VALUE OF
SELF-CONTROL

by
Sandra Lee Smith

THE ENCYCLOPEDIA OF
ETHICAL BEHAVIOR

THE ROSEN PUBLISHING GROUP, INC.
NEW YORK

Published in 1991 by The Rosen Publishing Group, Inc.
29 East 21st Street, New York, NY 10010

First Edition

Manufactured in the United States of America

Library of Congress Cataloging-in-Publication Data

Smith, Sandra Lee.
    The value of self-control / by Sandra Lee Smith.
        p.   cm.—(The Encyclopedia of ethical behavior)
    Includes bibliographical references and index.
    Summary: Defines self-control and discusses its importance
in developing moral and ethical behavior that is necessary for
an individual and a society to function effectively.
    ISBN 0-8239-1270-1
    1. Teenagers—Conduct of life.   2. Self-control.
[1. Conduct of life.   2. Self-control.]   I. Title.   II. Series.
BJ1661.S625   1991
179'.9—dc20
                                                                        90-44054
                                                                            CIP
                                                                            AC

Cover Photo: Courtesy of The Image Bank
All Other Photos: Wide World Photos

About the Author

For twenty-one years, Sandra Lee Smith has taught grades from kindergarten through college level in California and Arizona. Her extensive travels in Canada and Central and South America have included observations in public and private schools as well as teacher training programs.

As a consultant in connection with Arizona State University, where she obtained her M.A. in Bilingual/Multicultural Education, she has conducted workshops for teachers and parents throughout the Southwest.

Ms. Smith has been hired as a consultant by the Central Valley Teacher Education Center in California and the Bureau of Indian Affairs in New Mexico to teach aspects of the whole language process.

Active on legislative committees and in community projects, she has helped design programs to involve parents in the education process.

In response to the President's Report, *A Nation at Risk*, Ms. Smith participated in a project involving Arizona State University, Phoenix Elementary School District, and an inner-city community in Phoenix. Participants in the project developed a holistic approach to education that Ms. Smith and others successfully implemented in their classrooms; from their research and application, a whole language program emerged involving the three C's — Composition, Comprehension, and Critical Thinking.

To my niece, Julie Skidmore,
a young woman who practices admirable
self-control.

Contents

CHAPTER 1

What Is Self-control?

The Merriam-Webster dictionary defines *self* as: "1. *the essential person distinct from all other persons in identity*, 2. *a particular side of a person's character*, 3. *personal interest*."

The dictionary defines *control* as: "1. *power to direct or regulate*, 2. *reserve, restraint*, 3. *a device for regulating a mechanism*."

By definition, the combination *self-control* is the power to direct or regulate a person's identity, character, or personal interest. Most often it incorporates all three aspects of self, but at times it may apply only to one. Let's take personal interest for example. A football player has a game the next day. It is in his interest to go home from the party early and get plenty of rest. It is also in his personal interest not to drink before a game. He exerts self-control over his behavior to regulate his personal interest.

Another football player may not go to the party at all because he belongs to a religious sect that prohibits parties. He exerts self-control to regulate his character. He will not compromise his values to do something he considers wrong.

A third football player goes to the party but doesn't really enjoy parties. He would rather be walking on the beach with his girlfriend. He goes to the party because it is expected of him. He exerts self-control to preserve his identity.

Self-control is valued in most societies. If you were the only human being on an island, you could live without it. You could do what you pleased and not affect anyone. Your identity and your character would not be questioned, so you would not need self-control.

The famous quotation from John Donne: "No man is an island unto himself" expresses the need for self-control. We need to identify who we are and to develop character to maintain personal interest. Lack of self-control leads to anarchy, chaos, and ultimately self-destruction. Let's examine exactly what self-control is.

SELF-CONTROL IS — MORALITY

Morality is moral conduct or conformance to a standard of behavior. Every society has rules by which the members of that society are expected to live. The standard of behavior that a population establishes becomes a culture. From infancy we are taught to conform to that culture or set of rules.

The rules in a culture are laid out as laws. Large cultures establish governments to enforce those laws. Smaller cultures have designated members such as elders, counselors, priests, or shamans to regulate behavior.

Besides formal rules or laws, cultures have subtle patterns of behavior that members are expected to follow. Such values as honesty, fairness, and truth are taught within the framework of the family.

Manners or social contact between people is another subtle pattern of right behavior. We learn early the correct way to approach strangers. We are taught how to speak to elders. We learn not only what to say, but the tone of voice to use, the physical body language that goes with it, and even the distance to stand from a person when talking.

In some cultures it is rude to stand close to a stranger. In others it is rude not to. In the United States we extend a greeting with a handshake of our right hand. In Arabic countries that action is an insult.

In a small Greek community, the priest has a strong influence on the behavior of the people.

Moral behavior is taught from infancy. By the age of four most of us are aware of the subtle and the overt standards of behavior we are expected to follow. That means that most of morality is taught and learned in the home. It is important for families to interact and help the young to develop patterns of right behavior.

This right behavior is determined by self-control. A person may be taught all the rules and expected behavior of his society, but that does not mean he can be forced to obey them. Each person decides how much self-control he or she will exert.

Honesty may be the expected moral behavior, but you decide how honest you will be. Sometimes we are honest with our family but not with teachers. Sometimes we are honest when with our religious leaders but not at home. The degree of honesty we practice is determined by self-control.

We are disciplined from infancy to be moral. Not being moral usually has consequences. If we tell a lie and are caught, we are punished. The consequences of our actions determine how much self-control we decide to use.

In most cultures murder or theft brings severe punishment. Because of that, most people restrain themselves from committing those crimes. The more subtle morality is more difficult to define, and thus the consequences are less drastic. Cheating on a test will not put you in jail. You might be more tempted to cheat than to steal.

How you perceive the consequences determines how much self-control you exert. If you want to be considered a moral citizen of your community, you will strive to conform to the standards of behavior acceptable to that society. You will be self-controlled.

SELF-CONTROL IS — HONESTY

Truth is the real state of things, the body of real events or facts, and the agreement with fact or reality. Honesty is being truthful or free from deception. An honest person is marked by integrity.

Nobody can make a person truthful. A person is honest because he or she decides to be. Several outside conditions may exist that make it more desirable to be honest than dishonest. For example, you might prefer to tell the truth rather than be punished by your parents.

As we noted earlier, cultures and societies have set standards of behavior. The rules become your reality. Being honest means conforming to your reality. If honesty in your culture means that you may not ask a friend for help on a test, then to be honest you must exert self-control and not ask for the answers even if you want or need to.

Not every culture has the same standards. Some cultures

would consider it immoral not to help a friend on the test. In the Navajo nation it is considered dishonest to try to do better on a test than your friends. The way to act is to help your friends.

These differences in the way cultures perceive honesty or any other moral behavior make it difficult for us to learn self-control. When we live in a country that has many different cultures, we sometimes become confused. We may not really know what "self" we are.

Take a Navajo student for example. He lives in two cultures with different definitions of honesty. Choosing which one to live by is bound to be a problem.

If we live in a well-defined culture, we know what behavior is expected of us. That makes it easier to be self-controlled. The next step is acting on that knowledge.

If you are at a McDonald's with your friends and the waitress gives you change for a twenty-dollar bill instead of the ten-dollar bill you gave her, what do you do?

You alone control your actions. What would make you decide to be honest and return the extra ten dollars? What would make you decide to keep it?

You would rely on past experience. Maybe you had a job on which you gave change and you made that mistake. If you had to make up the difference out of your pocket and you remember how painful that was, you may be more inclined to return the ten dollars to the waitress.

You would also rely on what you have been taught. If your family has rewarded you when you were honest, you might remember that and return the ten dollars. On the other hand, if you have seen your parents gloat when they received extra change, you might decide to keep it.

Your circumstances would also determine the degree of honesty you exert. If you have just cashed a paycheck and have plenty of money in your wallet, you might feel more inclined to be honest. But suppose your parents were both out of work and your baby brother was hungry. In that case you might be concerned about keeping the money, but your concern for your family would be greater.

Whatever decisions you make, and for whatever reasons, *you* control your degree of honesty.

SELF-CONTROL IS — BEING FAIR

Being fair involves conforming to the rules. It also entails unbiased and unprejudiced goodness. People who are considered fair have an objective attitude and treat others with honor.

Being fair is highly valued in any society. What *is* fair differs from one culture to another, but fairness is a virtue that has to be developed in each person.

To conform to the rules, you need to be clear on what the rules are. That makes learning self-control much easier. When you play soccer it is impossible to be fair unless you know the rules of the game. If you try to play as if it were football or hockey you'll run into protests from your team.

It works the same way in society. There are rules that we live by. They are needed because so many people living together would be confusing without restrictions and guidelines. If you don't know the rules or choose to ignore them, you could be considered unfair.

Take for example a girl who is waiting for a bus in Seattle. A family has been waiting longer. The bus arrives, and the family heads for it. Is it fair if the girl who has just arrived pushes her way up front and boards the bus ahead of the family? In Seattle that would be considered unfair.

If the girl were waiting for a bus in Mexico City, it would be a different matter. The rule there is to crowd onto the bus as fast as you can lest it leave without you. The girl would not be considered unfair or rude in Mexico.

Once you know the rules, you decide if you will follow them. The girl who waits for the family to board the bus first is practicing self-control. She is treating others with honor.

Being fair also means being without bias or prejudice. Again, knowing the rules helps, but you also need to know the circumstances. If you were from Seattle and visiting Mexico City, it would seem that the Mexicans were rude by crowding

The rules in a society are like the rules in a game: you have to understand them in order to be fair.

in front of you onto the bus. By not knowing their rules, you would be unfair in judging them.

To be fair, you not only need to be self-controlled, you need to be informed. In rural or small communities the mode of behavior is usually clearly defined. Large, complex societies contain too many cultures and environments to know them all. When rules and expected behavior are confusing, it is easy to fall into the trap of believing that life is unfair.

To avoid this pitfall, it is important to simplify your life. Decide what is important to you, and know the rules to achieve it. Then it becomes easier to be fair and self-controlled.

It helps to have goals and to work toward clear objectives. With those in your mind, it is easier to decide what behavior to practice.

As an example, suppose you are visiting Mexico City. If your goal is just to pass through, you won't take time to learn rules nor to judge fairly. If you want to learn about Mexican culture and plan to go to school there as an exchange student, your goals will demand that you learn the rules of Mexican culture and conform to them.

You will be safer by following the rules. You will be happier if you treat situations without prejudice. The decision to be fair, however, is still yours.

SELF-CONTROL IS — MANNERS

Manners are customary ways of acting. Manners involve social conduct. Most manners are subtle, and we learn polite behavior by watching how others act. Therefore, most of us learn manners from our family.

Some manners are taught later when you encounter different environments. You learn ways to act at school, in your religious community, and at work. Sometimes manners are spelled out in clear-cut rules. In school you may have to raise your hand to speak or sit without talking.

Manners may not be the same for each place. You need not raise your hand before speaking at home. If you work as a librarian you have to be silent, or you may be a teacher and have to talk.

Manners are not always the same for each setting. It is considered impolite in American culture to eat with your fingers at a formal dining table. Yet the same family or group of people may eat with their fingers at a picnic.

Besides clear-cut rules of behavior, manners include subtle ways of acting that are more difficult to define. For example, it is not polite to laugh when someone receives bad news. Or you are not rude to someone who has just complimented you. Can you think of other examples of subtle rules of social conduct?

These unwritten rules are not exactly taught. We learn them by responses of our elders or peers. For example, if you stand too close to someone from a culture that has a larger space requirement no one needs to tell you what you've done. You will know immediately by the reaction of the other person, who will probably frown and step back from you.

As another example, in France it is customary for male friends to greet each other with a hug and a kiss on each cheek. What would happen if you did that in the United States? Would anyone have to spell out the rule for you? People convey their knowledge of subtle manners in many ways. Conduct is one way, as we have seen. Another way is through gestures.

You probably know several gestures that give obvious messages: hand signals that insult and others like a wave that are a friendly greeting. Facial expressions such as smiles welcome or encourage, whereas frowns show displeasure.

Body language conveys messages too. If you turn slightly away from someone in a group, you can effectively shut that person out. Can you think of other ways of transmitting messages with your body?

Correct poses and gestures are not necessarily taught in a formal manner. People learn them by observing and interacting. No matter how you learn them, however, you are in control of how you use them. You can consciously express bad or good manners. You decide to shake hands with some-one you meet, or you decide to frown at someone you dislike.

Some manners are unconscious and done by force of habit. Most people automatically smile when someone smiles at them. Most people automatically face the person they are talking to. Some people automatically salute the flag. Even though these habits are automatic, they were learned. That means that you can change them by practicing self-control.

It is important to examine your manners. Reinforce those that are positive. Manners that harm you or others need to be changed. You can do that by regulating your behavior.

SELF-CONTROL IS — AVOIDING MALICIOUS GOSSIP

Gossip is a rumor or report of an intimate nature. A person who gossips is one who reveals personal or sensational facts. Malicious gossip is rumors or reports of ill will.

Gossip in itself is not generally harmful. Television and radio news, magazines, and newspapers report sensational facts every day. Good news lifts people's spirits and hopes. Most people like to keep informed of the world around them, so hearing these facts is considered useful.

Malicious gossip is an entirely different matter. Most societies have strict regulations against slander, libel, and perjury, for the obvious reason that telling falsehoods can be injurious to others. Malice creates mistrust and discontent. A community cannot function under those conditions; therefore it makes strict regulations.

For example, if the radio announcer in your community announced that the local department store was giving away merchandise, what would happen? If a track team accused its opponents of using drugs to increase speed, what would it do to the image of the team in question? Even if the evidence proves the statements false, there is already damage to credibility.

Obvious and public instances are easy to control. The real problem is subtle instances of malicious gossip. How many times today have you said something negative about another person? Think back to your conversations with family, friends, classmates, or coworkers. Be honest and consider, were there statements that would have been better left unsaid?

Talking about other people, places, or things is one of the major problems that societies face. It doesn't seem very harmful, but in fact it is one of the most destructive lacks of self-control practiced today.

Let's look at an example. Marsha and Cindy are friends. One day Marsha gets mad at Cindy because she won't double-date with Bob, a friend of Marsha's boyfriend who lives in a neighboring town. To get even, Marsha tells a few of their classmates that Cindy did go on the date and besides that had sex with Bob.

Some of the boys from Cindy's school hear this report and ask her out, expecting to have sex with her as well. Two of the dates work out well because Cindy informs them that she does not engage in sexual behavior and the boys accept her values. The third guy has problems of his own and cannot handle Cindy's rejection. He ends up raping her. Cindy presses charges and the fellow winds up in court.

That is an extreme case, but lies do tend to snowball into disaster. Can you think of incidents of malicious gossip that didn't seem so bad at first but became very harmful?

Malicious gossip is a negative force that breeds other negative forces. Cindy is going to have trouble trusting men. Future male acquaintances will be affected by the negativity of her attitude.

Follow the golden rule about gossip: *If you can't say something nice, say nothing at all.* Practice self-control and use your head before you speak.

SELF-CONTROL IS — AVOIDING OBSCENE LANGUAGE

Webster's dictionary defines obscene as *offensive to morality or decency, designed to incite to lust or depravity.*

When you use obscene language, are you aware that that is what you are doing? Most people swear because they are angry or frustrated. It is acceptable behavior to be angry sometimes, and surely everyone experiences frustration. But what do you accomplish by using obscene language?

Shouting releases some of the pent-up anger and frustration. It isn't the word you choose to use, but the physical release of shouting that relieves the tension. It is just as effective to shout "Darn," "Blast," or even "Cinnamon candy." Try it sometime.

It is wise to select your vocabulary to reflect the self-image you wish to project. Consider carefully the definition of *obscene*. Doesn't it seem ridiculous for someone to stub his toe and shout obscenities *designed to incite to lust or depravity*?

Unfortunately, much of the media use obscene language. Often the movies use it appropriately when characters in the plot intend to *incite to lust or depravity*. But because it is used in a movie does not make it okay to use obscene language at inappropriate times.

For obscene language to have real impact, it must be used sparingly and at the proper time. Overuse makes it ineffective as well as offensive. It tells others that you lack self-control in not saving the language for the appropriate time.

Obscene language is also used to *offend morality or decency*. Some people swear to insult others. Can you think of incidents when you have used obscene language for that purpose? Consider the pros and cons of each incident. What were the benefits of swearing at that person? Did it relieve tension? Did you feel happy, and was the happiness true joy or perhaps vengeful glee? Did you gain anything by swearing?

Now look at the negative effects. Did you create greater dissension? How did the other person react? Did it solve the problem?

Sometimes people fall into the habit of using obscene language, especially if family or friends do so often. Habits can be changed. The ultimate person who controls what you say is *you*.

Remember the definition of self-control? It reflects your character and identity. Consider how you want to be viewed by your society. Your language lets the world know what type of person you are. If you constantly use obscene language you will be considered a person who is *inciting to lust or depravity*.

If that is not your intention and you use obscene language anyway, you appear ignorant of your purpose. It is misuse of language, like saying "I have two feets" or "Her has the car now."

Another factor in considering the image you want to portray is what you want to accomplish in life. If you want steady employment, a happy home, and good friends, you must learn

In a large city, breaking the rules may seem more tempting because people feel anonymous.

to control your language. No employer, spouse, or friend will want to associate with someone who is *offensive to morality or decency.*

SELF-CONTROL IS — CURBING ANGER

Anger is a strong feeling of displeasure. It includes the emotions of wrath, ire, and rage.

Anger is a natural emotion that everyone experiences. When you live with other people it is necessary to let them know when they do something that you disapprove of or resent. If something makes you unhappy, you may need to express anger in order to make others aware. Awareness is necessary for change.

Disapproving anger is used to socialize persons to the rules of the society. When you were little, your parents became angry when you broke toys or hit your brother or sister. Their anger let you know that the behavior was not acceptable.

Anger is also an emotion that is necessary to socialize a community. A society must get angry if its rules are broken; otherwise people would break rules all the time, knowing that they would not be punished.

That is why it is more difficult to break rules in a small community. Everyone knows pretty much what others are doing. A person cannot break the rules without incurring the community's wrath and punishment.

In a large city people are more anonymous. An individual can behave more freely because the likelihood of anyone's knowing or caring what he is doing is slim. Because no one knows or cares, no one is angry when the person does not obey a law.

Because of the absence of punishment, the person is more likely to break the law unless he or she practices self-control. That is why the crime rates in cities are higher than in rural areas and why overpopulated areas experience chaos and anarchy.

Excessive anger or anger that is not under control can be extremely harmful. Parents who punish their child are teaching behavior. Parents who have no control of their anger abuse the child.

Many situations arise that cause anger, but society would be in chaos if it were not controlled. Definite limits are placed on how much anger is allowed to be expressed. You have control of your emotions and must learn ways to restrain the anger that is churning inside of you. You need to control your anger for society's benefit and for your own.

Anger that dwells within you can lead to emotional stress. You must find ways to release it safely or it can develop into rage and hatred. Anger that is contained creates chemicals in your body that will eventually make you ill. Ulcers, cancer, and heart disease are often engendered by anger. Nervous breakdown, hyperactivity, and depression are also caused by pent-up anger.

Psychologists suggest many constructive ways to release

anger. Exercise is always effective. Instead of hitting someone, have a few rounds with a punching bag. Running laps blows off steam. Swimming, bicycling, and other aerobic exercise help to relieve stress.

It is possible and necessary to control anger. Use it constructively, and learn to release it.

SELF-CONTROL IS — NOT PERMITTING JEALOUSY

Jealousy is demanding complete devotion. A jealous person is one who is suspicious of a rival or of one believed to enjoy an advantage.

Most people experience jealousy in some form. Self-interest makes us want to be the most important human being in our circle of acquaintances. It is natural to want a person's complete devotion, but it is also unrealistic. Every person interacts with more than one other person. You have to give something of yourself to those you encounter, even if it is simply a greeting or a nod.

It is undesirable in communities to isolate individuals. We are social beings and need to interact with others. If nothing else, we rely on others for necessities. Few hermits exist who can supply all their own needs.

Not only do people desire full attention, they also desire what others have that they don't. For example, if your friend has a lot of girlfriends and you don't, you can easily become jealous of him. If your sister can go out on dates and you can't, it is natural to be jealous. Can you think of people you are jealous of? Why?

Jealousy, if kept in control, won't harm you. In fact, it helps you focus on your goals. If you want what someone else has, you will strive toward getting it.

Jealousy if not controlled can be extremely harmful. Receiving complete attention from a girlfriend or boyfriend is impossible. That partner must interact with others to remain emotionally and physically healthy. If you react with jealousy, you can damage your relationship, your partner, and yourself.

Take the young man whose friend has all the girlfriends for an example. If he doesn't control his jealousy, he will begin to behave in an antisocial manner toward his friend. It may not be bad enough to lose that friend, but what was he jealous of? Girlfriends, right? Do you think girls are going to be interested in him if he acts antisocially?

What about the girl who is jealous because her sister can go on dates. If she throws a tantrum, will her parents smile and say, "Sure, honey, you can go on a date"? Those parents are going to see the tantrum and realize that this child is too immature to date.

It is important to control feelings of jealousy. They can be harmful to you as well as damaging to your social life. Jealousy held within acts like anger; it can release chemical reactions that cause cancer, ulcers, and nervous disorders. Emotional imbalance also occurs. Uncontrolled jealousy can lead to depression, violent behavior, and stress.

The same ways of dealing with anger apply to jealousy. Physical exercise is always beneficial. Sometimes talking to a family member, a close friend, or a counselor helps. Experts can suggest solutions that fit your particular problem.

Learn to take advantage of your emotions. Identify what is making you jealous. Then use your energy to attain what you are jealous of.

For example, the girl who wants to go on dates can plan projects that will prove to her parents that she is mature. That approach would be much more effective than the tantrum.

Because jealousy is an emotion, you *can* control it. It is important to do so to function as a healthy and happy citizen of your community.

SELF-CONTROL IS — RESISTING ENVY

Envy is a grudging desire for or discontent at the sight of another's advantages.

In all the history of mankind, envy is probably the single

By taking steroids, Ben Johnson destroyed his Olympic career.

factor that most contributes to problems, discontent, and war. Whenever a person, society, or nation wants what another has and wants it to the point of doing anything to get it, you have strife.

Like jealousy, envy to a small degree will not harm you. It can inspire you to set goals so that you can achieve what you envy. Star athletes practice so that they can win awards. School teams and sports exist because the community covets the championship.

In class you study to earn top grades. At work you exert yourself so that you will be rewarded with promotion.

These are all results of envy or desiring something someone else has. If you control it, it can work for you. The problem with envy is that it can easily end up controlling you.

For example, let's look at a track star who wants the Gold Medal so much that she gives up family relationships to have time to practice. She never helps with family chores and is never there when she is needed. She even risks her health by taking steroids to enable her to run faster.

That kind of obsession can destroy a person. Similar cases have occurred among Olympic athletes. Most Olympic stars, however, become so because they practice self-control and discipline their lives.

Other examples of control by envy are a person who wants outstanding grades so much that he cheats on tests; or one who wants to dress like her friends but has no money to buy clothes, so she steals them; or one who wants to be "in" and thinks taking drugs will make him so. Can you think of other instances?

Envy can make you want something to the point that you will do anything to get it, even if it is against your values. Sometimes envy works in another way to destroy you. If you see no way to get what someone else has, you may become discontented. Discontent means unhappiness. This unhappiness can build until it destroys you or others.

Examples are seen in situations of racial prejudice. Say a black student wants to join the country club. He loves to play golf and in fact is quite good at it, having learned in summers that he spent with his uncle, a pro golfer.

Unfortunately, the country club will not allow blacks to join.

There is nothing the student can do about his skin color, but he does have choices. He can find a way to resolve the problem, or he can let bitterness, anger, and envy eat away at him until he is as full of hatred as the bigots at the country club.

Which will benefit him the most? He can use the envy to fight for civil rights at the country club. He can look for another club. He can dream about building his own club.

Or he can let envy control him by allowing bitterness and anger to fester inside him. This can lead to physical stress, illness, nervous breakdown. Hatred also taints relationships with others. Do you like to be around someone who is full of bitterness?

What other options does this student have?

You have the power to decide how much control you exert over envy. You can decide how wanting something will affect your life. Envy can control you and eventually destroy you, or you can control it and use it to your advantage.

SELF-CONTROL IS — MODERATION

To practice moderation is to lessen the intensity of your behavior. It requires self-discipline and mastery of your emotions. When a person acts or reacts in moderation, he or she is calm and stable. A stable person is mentally healthy and well balanced.

Persons who do not practice moderation can easily be identified. They stand out in the crowd because they take things to extremes. A show-off is carried away with the way he acts, and we notice him; he might be loud, boisterous, or rowdy.

Persons who have had too much to drink are noticed because they walk or talk strangely or become disoriented and violent. If they drive, shoot firearms, or operate heavy equipment in this condition, they become dangerous to themselves and others.

People who eat too much make themselves obvious because their lack of moderation leads to weight problems.

Sexual promiscuity is another example of lack of moderation. This lack of self-control may or may not be obvious to others; however, if unwanted pregnancy results it is a problem that affects many lives.

Moderation in simple terms is learning to say no. It is one of the most important aspects of self-control because it can affect your survival. It is a universal law that anything carried to an extreme creates an imbalance. When that happens, the results can be life-threatening to you or others.

If you lack self-control in areas such as honesty, manners, and fairness, you will not necessarily harm yourself or another. You may be unpopular or you may be avoided, laughed at, or scolded, but those consequences are not drastic when compared to lack of moderation.

The major problems that teens face regarding moderation are drinking, eating, using drugs, and engaging in sexual immorality. Carrying any of those to extremes can and does lead to serious threats to life.

The main consideration you must face in these areas is whether you want to live or die. If you choose life, you must decide what quality of life you want to enjoy.

If it is important to you to be physically fit, you may decide to be concerned about how much you eat or drink. If impressing or submitting to peers is not important to you because of your integrity and self-identity, you will choose not to practice sexual promiscuity with uncommitted partners. If you want to solve unbearable problems, you will not try to escape through drugs.

The important thing to remember is that none of these areas has to be out of your control. They will be so only if *you* allow it. You decide whether you will use restraint in your actions, whether you will abstain from eating that chocolate sundae or drinking another beer.

If you do not believe you can say no, seek help. There are counselors at school and in religious organizations and community services.

Many large cities have crisis centers, telephone hotlines, and emergency aides. Seek out these people if your life is in

Extreme lack of self-control can lead to alarming health problems.

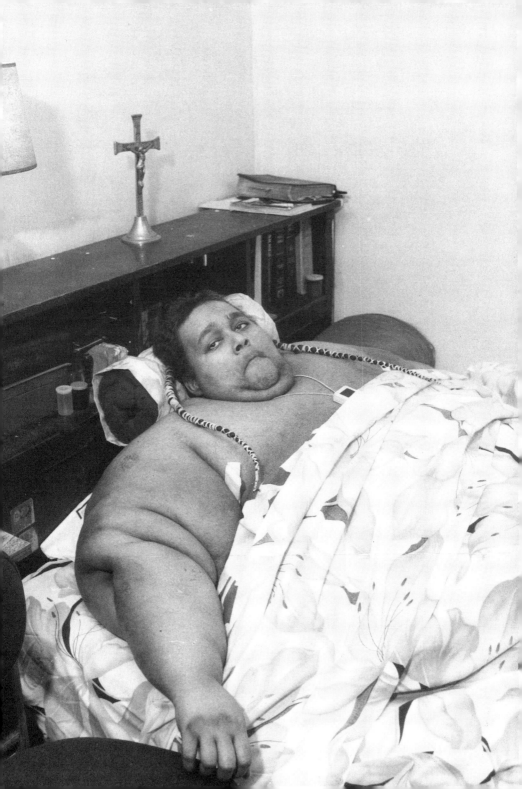

danger. You can learn to be moderate and gain back your self-control.

SELF-CONTROL IS — FORGIVING

To forgive is to give up resentment or to grant relief of payment. Granting relief of payment could mean actual monetary debts or emotional debts such as revenge, insult, war. It could be a debt against society such as a crime, or a debt against your religion such as a sin.

Forgiveness means canceling those debts. It means making peace or granting pardon. The result of forgiveness is erasing the debt from your memory and giving you a sense of peace.

Everyone wants peace, but most people find it difficult to release those feelings of resentment or to cancel debts. If someone harms you, it takes tremendous self-control not to react in the negative way of revenge. It takes even more self-control to forgive.

Forgiving is one of the hardest things to do, yet once done it can be the most rewarding. When you don't forgive, you not only harm the person or group involved, but in fact you can harm yourself more.

Few people realize how self-destructive unforgiveness is. If you hate or resent someone those emotions cause chemical imbalances in your body that lead to stress, physical illness, and psychological breakdown.

Forgiveness on the other hand frees you of all of that ugliness. When you are not thinking about how much you hate someone, it frees your mind to think about how much you like someone else.

Let's look at Darlene and Sarah. They are close friends and do things together all the time, but there is a problem. Sarah is also friends with Tammy. Darlene dislikes Tammy because Tammy spread malicious gossip about Darlene's brother.

Darlene can handle this in several ways. If she chooses to be unforgiving, she must decide what to do about her friendship with Sarah. Will she avoid Sarah? Will she complain about Tammy to Sarah? Will she say spiteful things to Tammy? You can probably think of several ways Darlene can act in an unforgiving manner.

Consider Tammy and Sarah. If Darlene acts that way, what will Tammy and Sarah do? What would you do? Darlene will probably lose Sarah's friendship. No one likes to be caught in the middle of a feud, especially if they like both parties.

If that happens, who suffers the most? Why?

Let's look at it another way. Suppose Darlene really values Sarah's friendship. She doesn't like what Tammy did, but she knows that Tammy is Sarah's friend. Perhaps Darlene has a talk with Tammy and tells her that she doesn't like what Tammy said about her brother. Tammy apologizes. Darlene forgives her, and the matter is dropped.

What will be the results of that action? What other ways could Darlene forgive Tammy? Do you think Darlene will be happier?

Remember that you make the decision to forgive. You must live with the consequences. Also remember that you will be the one who benefits the most from your forgiveness.

Think now about people you have not forgiven. How has that affected your life? Give each case an honest appraisal and see whether you would not be happier by forgiving them. It is your choice. Forgiveness is under your control to grant.

SELF-CONTROL IS — GENEROSITY

Generosity is freely giving or sharing. A generous person is high-minded.

The opposite value of envy, jealousy, anger, and unforgiveness is generosity. Instead of coveting objects, people, or feelings, a generous person freely gives them away.

Most cultures value generosity because it leads to peace and harmony, something every culture strives for. Since a society is made up of many individuals, the society needs to remain peaceful to survive. That is why it sets values. Generosity is highly prized.

Most philosophies dwell on the law of generosity and determine that the more generous you are, the more generosity you will receive. Think about why that is so.

If you have a friend who always offers you treats, cookies, candies, flowers, good books, don't you want to find things that please that friend and offer a gift also? How often have you been surprised when a friend gave you something he or she valued? How do you react to such people?

We can be generous with more than objects. We have seen how jealousy destroys. Think how rewarding your friendships are if you share them with others.

Emotions can also be shared. A person who is generous with compliments usually receives them in turn. A person who takes the time to comfort friends who are hurting usually has friends to comfort him in time of trouble.

A friend who invites people into his home to share meals and hospitality usually has many invitations. A friend who is warmhearted rarely is treated with disrespect.

Can you think of other instances of generosity and the results?

You control the degree of generosity you dispense. Because there is a direct relationship between how much generosity you give and how much you receive, you need to evaluate your life carefully.

What exactly do you want? Think of objects first. If you want more clothes, give the old ones away. If you want more tape cassettes, give some away. If you want money, give it away. It doesn't seem to make sense, but try it and see if it doesn't work. Remember, you have to be patient, as the results do not come overnight.

If you are hesitant to try it yourself, look at people you admire. Notice what they have in abundance. It is usually something they freely give. Study the successful people in your community. Most wealthy business people donate money or services or both. Famous doctors provide free services to the poor. Actors and singers perform for charities. Most of these people will tell you that generosity not only contributes to their abundance, but it makes them feel good as well.

Your degree of generosity does not depend on how much money you have. There are many ways to be generous. Can you list them?

Many famous musicians donated time and talent at the Live Aid Famine Relief Concert.

The important thing to remember is that you control how generous you will be.

SELF-CONTROL IS — PATIENCE

Patience is the capacity, habit, or fact of being patient. To be patient is to bear pain or trials without complaint. Patience is showing self-control. A patient person is calm, steadfast, and persevering.

In all the areas of self-control, patience is the one that can slip away without a person's realizing it. You can have all the good intentions in the world, but a situation will come up and suddenly patience disappears.

Life is full of trials. There will never be a time when you won't have to face them. Therefore, it is important to learn to bear them without complaint. Impatience will not get rid of the pain or trials. What will is your control over them.

Suppose you are waiting to get your driver's license. It is two months until your birthday. After that you won't have to beg rides from your brother, you won't have to depend on someone else, and best of all, you'll be able to take your girlfriend out on dates alone. Two months seems forever. What will that wait be like if you are impatient? Will impatience make the time go faster? How will the time pass if you are patient?

Impatience rarely works toward solving the problem. Patience doesn't always solve the problem either, but it makes it easier to bear. Patience didn't make the two months pass faster but it did make you more pleasant to be around and a happier person.

Let's look at Donna and Michelle. They want to go to the movies but first have to help their mom put their younger sisters to bed. In her rush, Donna puts the baby's nightie on backwards and has to stop and change it. She bumps into the toychest, spills the toys, and has to stop and pick them up. While getting dressed she pulls on her skirt too quickly and rips it. Now she has to stop and mend it.

Michelle on the other hand stays calm and is patient with her two-year-old sister, Roxy. Michelle smiles at the child, and because Roxy is content she cooperates when Michelle changes her into pajamas. Roxy crawls into bed without a fuss, and Michelle even has time to read a story while Donna is picking up toys.

While Donna mends her skirt, Michelle has time to help her mother with the dinner dishes. That makes mom so happy that she treats the girls to their tickets to the movies.

Imagine how the scenario would change if Donna had control of her patience. What would have happened if Michelle had not been patient?

Can you think of situations in your life when you did not have patience? Think what would have changed if you had been patient.

Patience is another factor you can control. You not only have the capacity to be patient, but you can develop it into a habit. Some people consciously count to ten before they make decisions or speak out. Others find ways to develop patience by talking to peers, parents, counselors, or religious teachers.

Patience makes you a happier person, and it makes those around you happy. How did Roxy respond to Michelle's patience? Whom would you rather be around, Donna or Michelle?

Patience *is* self-control. You can have as much of it as you decide to have.

SELF-CONTROL IS — COMPASSION

Compassion is a feeling of sympathy and a desire to alleviate distress. A compassionate person is kind, merciful, warm-hearted, and humane.

Self-control is an essential tool for getting along with others in a family, community, and culture. Self-control is not so vital when living alone. It has to do with relationships with others.

Interacting with others is of primary importance to survival. Almost every culture values compassion as an important tool in doing so.

Human beings were not designed to be perfect. We have free will. We can choose who and what we are. Because of that we make mistakes.

If you can understand that basic premise, you can develop compassion. There is an old saying, "Honey catches more flies than vinegar." Can you relate that saying to compassion?

Let's look at Paul. He has volunteered to help the baseball team with their equipment. Part of his responsibility is to bring up the bat each hitter likes to use when he comes to bat. Other jobs are to bring the players drinks, get wet towels for them, and collect their caps.

One day Paul is having a rough time of it. His mother is ill, and he's worried about her. Consequently his mind isn't fully on the ball game. It's Jim's turn to bat, and Paul hands him the wrong bat.

"What the heck's wrong with you?" Jim throws the bat and yells at Paul.

Kevin is up next, and Paul hands him the wrong bat too. By

now Paul is very upset. Kevin gets his bat and smiles at Paul.

"It's okay. I've got it," he says.

Later Kevin asks Paul what is the trouble. He offers to help Paul straighten up the gym after the game so that Paul can get home early.

Which player was compassionate and how? What do you think Paul thought about each player? Kevin's sympathy and support helped him through a tough time.

Now consider future ball games. Compare the treatment Kevin will get from Paul with that of Jim.

Have you ever asked your parents if you could go to a movie or shopping with a friend and had them blow up with anger? Sharon did. She wanted to go shopping, but when she asked permission her mother lost her self-control and started yelling.

"You always want to go shopping. You're never at home. All you do is spend money."

A self-centered person might argue with her mother. An angry person might yell back. But a compassionate person might read her mother's feelings in her mother's statements. Maybe she had had a bad day. Maybe bills were due and finances were tight. Maybe she was lonely and didn't want Sharon to leave.

What do you think a compassionate person could do in this situation? Yelling at her mother surely won't accomplish anything. Always remember the honey and the vinegar.

Having compassion often means putting your own interests on hold while you help someone out. Again, it is your choice to develop it or not. You have control of how you treat others. You decide whether you will feel kind, merciful, tender, or warmhearted.

To be humane is to consider your fellow man. Living in a community and culture is much easier, happier, and more peaceful if you develop a compassionate nature.

CHAPTER 2

History of Self-control

Man has practiced self-control since he began. He is a being with free will. Therefore, to function within a society or culture he has to learn to control his wants and needs so that they conform. Conformity is necessary so that people within a culture can interact peacefully. It is necessary to insure survival. In all instances where man did not practice self-control, the result has been death.

Some societies have very strict laws. Other laws are less well defined. In any case, it isn't how strict the laws are that makes you practice self-control, it is the control you decide to exert.

In the Bible, Adam did not practice wise self-control. He had a choice, he knew the consequence, yet he did what he was not supposed to do. There is no harsher punishment than death. It wasn't the punishment that controlled Adam; it was himself.

In history, civilizations have established rules or laws. Breaking those laws always brings punishment or consequences, yet there will always be someone who chooses to break them.

That is not always bad. Some laws are so restrictive or unfair that it takes a courageous person to get them changed. That person exerts self-control by suffering the consequences and punishments to prove the points.

All the heroes throughout the ages have practiced various forms of self-control. Columbus overcame fear and uncertainty to travel across the ocean and land in the New World. There he found peoples who had their own cultures and rules of control.

The Spanish explorers were welcomed by Montezuma because he practiced generosity and compassion to weary travelers, forms of self-control that were encouraged in his society. We know that Montezuma regretted his courtesy, but he was making decisions relative to his culture and times. He had no way of knowing that the Spanish conquistadors would lose their self-control and destroy the Aztec civilization because of envy and greed.

It was not only heroes who practiced self-control. No matter where a person lives, every man or woman has to make the decision to follow rules, conform to the culture, or try to make change. Every person has free will to decide how much self-control he or she exerts.

The Anasazi, the Arapaho, and the Sioux all had cultural standards by which they lived. They valued the harmony between man and the land. They did not believe that people could own land, and they had no desire to do so.

European settlers who invaded the territories brought conflict because they were operating on a different set of values. They valued land and wanted to own it and use it for their own gain.

Conflict occurred because of the difference in values. However, in instances where Native Americans and settlers practiced self-control and used compassion, forgiveness, fairness, and manners, they were able to develop peaceful interaction.

For many years European explorers and traders lived among American natives and traded furs and game for trinkets and tools. It was when the European settlers lost their self-control that imbalance and disharmony occurred. They told lies about the Indians. They let greed and envy control them to the point that they destroyed a whole race of people for material gain.

History shows more cases of loss of self-control than of practice of self-control. If you study peaceful periods of history, you will see the majority of the population practicing self-control. It leads to peace and harmony.

If there is greed, famine, and dissension, you will see a majority of the population with a lack of self-control. This creates war and destruction. Remember that all wars are basically concerned with a culture or society wanting something another culture or society has.

The Spanish destroyed the Aztecs and the Incas for gold. European settlers killed Native Americans for land. The Civil War was a battle over slaves and human rights. World Wars I and II were struggles for power.

Can you think of historical characters who exemplify the practice of self-control. Historical characters who do not?

One of the outstanding American figures who embodied many of the aspects of self-control was Dr. Martin Luther King, Jr., a black minister who tried very hard in his public image to be moral, honest, and fair. He did not always succeed, but his successes outshone his failures.

Dr. King did not see himself the way his community did. He was the son of a Baptist minister, and he listened to his father preach. In the sermons he heard promises of human rights and human dignity. He learned about brotherly love, compassion, and forgiveness.

Those concepts sounded good, but they were not what he experienced. In the rural South he saw blacks treated with discrimination, hatred, and unfairness. That did not agree with his personal identity nor his character nor his personal interest.

He determined to make change and bring the reality up to the ideal of what black men and women had a right to be.

Young Martin was exceptionally bright. He knew he would have to go to school and learn before he could help people. That took self-control, especially since blacks in those days often had to quit school and go to work to help support their family.

Martin had feelings of envy. He wanted what white Americans had: better jobs, education, and a better standard of living. Many of his peers turned that envy into hatred, jealousy, and anger. These emotions became self-destructive, and many turned to alcohol to forget.

Martin channeled his energies of envy into constructive projects. He graduated from high school at the age of fifteen

after skipping several grades. Imagine the self-control required to do all that studying. He was able to do it because he had goals. He had a dream.

Martin was also a "good talker." He said it was because he was small for his age and had to talk himself out of trouble rather than fight. As a junior in high school he was on the debating team. An incident on the way home from a debate shaped his life and was another example of his self-control.

His team had won second place and were excited and proud. They were making the ninety-mile trip home by bus. Martin and a friend were sitting in the front of the bus, although in those days blacks were supposed to sit in the back. At a stop some white people got on the bus. All the seats were taken, and the driver asked Martin and his friend to give up their seats.

At first Martin refused. He figured he had just as much right to sit there as the whites did. In his eyes, this was not the way to treat debate winners. It took self-control not to react to his anger. It took self-control for him to stand on his ideals of fairness. Yet when his teacher, whom he admired, became uncomfortable and agitated, his compassion for her took over and he gave up the seats. That meant that he and his friend had to stand for ninety miles.

What would you have done in Martin's situation? Would you have had the self-control he did?

Martin attended Morehouse College. It was while there that he decided on his profession. He knew he wanted to help people, and he was considering being a doctor or a lawyer. But at this time he read Henry David Thoreau's essay on "Civil Disobedience." Thoreau had refused to cooperate with unjust laws.

Martin read and reread the essay, and he realized that Thoreau's technique might be used to help blacks fight the unfair discrimination in the South. As a sociology major, he also realized that he would need to reach a lot of people to teach that kind of thinking.

Dr. Martin Luther King advocated using self-control in the form of nonviolent resistance to correct problems in society.

With these considerations in mind, Martin Luther King decided to become a minister. At seventeen he preached his first sermon and knew that this was how he was going to help his people.

After graduation as a minister from Morehouse, an all-black college in Atlanta, he went to Crozer Theological Seminary in Chester, Pennsylvania. That was the first time he went to school with whites.

The North did not enforce all the restrictions that existed in the South, such as separate drinking fountains, bathrooms, and seating on buses for whites and blacks. But he did notice a different kind of prejudice, more subtle yet just as unfair. Blacks in the north lived in slums, and if they had jobs they received lower salaries.

While at Crozer, Martin heard a lecture about Mohandas Gandhi and his methods of nonviolence for change. Gandhi's theories of resisting British rule in India intrigued Martin. He saw that nonviolent protest marches and boycotts would be a way for black America to exert change without bending his standards of morality. He would be able to combine his teachings of Christianity and the ideas of Thoreau and Gandhi. "Rebel against unjust laws with love."

Instead of rushing out to put his ideas into practice, Martin continued his schooling. He received a doctoral degree from Boston University. Do you think this is a measure of self-control? How?

Dr. King's first pastorate was a church in Montgomery, Alabama. It was there that the civil rights movement began in 1954.

Rosa Parks was riding a bus home from work and was told to stand for a white passenger. She refused to get up and did not budge until the police were called and she was arrested. Think of the self-control that act required. Rosa Parks defied all the Jim Crow laws of the culture she lived in.

Dr. King met with civil rights activists and several church

The Indian leader Mohandas Gandhi inspired many with his nonviolent methods of protest. Here at age 78 he fasts for peace.

ministers. They decided to speak to their congregations about boycotting the buses on Monday morning. On December 5, 1954, the first nonviolent protest occurred.

During the whole campaign Dr. King urged people to practice self-control. "Love must be our regulating ideal," he said. Many people tried to incite violence by throwing things at the protesters. A bomb was thrown on Dr. King's porch. Malicious gossip was spread that Dr. King was using the boycott association's money to buy a Cadillac. Again Dr. King exerted self-control by urging his association not to respond with violence.

Many people during that period did not practice self-control. They let anger, hatred, obscene language, and malicious talk control them. Looking back, however, it was those who practiced patience, forgiveness, compassion, and fairness who gained in the end.

After a year of struggle, the Supreme Court of the United States ruled that it was against constitutional law to force blacks to sit in the back of buses. Blacks were now permitted to enjoy the privileges that other Americans had. In theory, Dr. King was not fighting against American morality but working to make it apply to *all* Americans.

That victory led to nonviolent protests against abuse of other civil rights. A new organization was formed, the Southern Christian Leadership Conference, which worked to desegregate restaurants, schools, and places of employment.

Unfortunately, not all of Dr. King's followers managed enough self-control to remain nonviolent. Picture yourself doing so as people threw rocks at you or hurled nasty comments. It is man's nature to react to threats in a violent manner.

These eruptions of violence hurt Dr. King's cause. He, however, remained a forgiving man. Once while he was in New York autographing his book, *Stride Toward Freedom*, a woman stabbed him with a letter opener and injured him seriously. He realized that she was insane and did not press charges.

Dr. King was also a generous man. Often he spent his own money to help others. He spent much time on Freedom Rides and marches, even sacrificing time with his family. He committed all of his energies to helping others.

Martin Luther King dedicated time and energy to fighting racial injustice in America. Here he leads a civil rights march in Memphis.

All that required tremendous self-control. Dr. King was an exceptional man. Not everyone can live as he did, but by practicing self-control you can attain some of those attributes.

Nonviolent protests and boycotts such as those practiced by Gandhi and Dr. King demanded exceptional self-control. These two men were leaders, but both had thousands of followers who practiced what they preached. The self-control they exerted brought the success of the peace movement.

Personal success was Dr. King's as well. In 1963 he was named Man of the Year by *Time* magazine. He also received several honorary degrees, including a Doctor of Laws from Yale University.

President John F. Kennedy asked Dr. King to help him draft a Civil Rights Bill. Before the President was assassinated, he presented the bill to Congress, and in 1964 President Johnson signed it into law.

On October 14, 1964, Dr. King was honored with the Nobel Peace Prize. At thirty-five he was the youngest person ever to receive the award. He was the second American black to receive it.

At the award ceremony Dr. King showed another aspect of self-control. He did not take full credit for all that had been accomplished, but generously acknowledged the thousands of blacks and whites who had worked with him toward civil rights. Furthermore he donated the large cash prize to the civil rights movement.

Dr. Martin Luther King, Jr. was a man who had a dream. He worked hard and used self-control to achieve it.

CHAPTER 3

Self-control In Today's Life

We have seen how self-control or lack of it affected history. Self-control is valued just as much in today's world. The problem with today's world is that it is very complex. Our American culture is a blend of many cultures. Many of you live in cities and large communities. Those factors make our values difficult to define.

If morals, manners, a sense of fairness, and a sense of honor are not clearly established, it is difficult to know what self-control entails.

Families that have immigrated from another country may practice one set of values at home. The parents go to work and practice another set of values there. The children are expected to attend school and follow that behavior pattern.

Even families who have been American for generations have difficulty because the United States is a nation of change. By the time you learn a set of values or a pattern of behavior, it is outdated and you must move on to a new one.

Another problem with establishing self-control in today's world occurs in urban areas. So many people are busy living their own lives and worrying about their own society that they tend to ignore behavior that doesn't fit within the rules. If no one cares that you are not practicing self-control and conforming to the rules, the temptation to do what you please is intensified.

Self-control is still valued in our complex society. In this chapter we shall look at the environments that require self-control and see if we can identify the need for it.

SELF-CONTROL IN THE HOME

Self-control is learned from infancy. Since the definition of self-control includes personal identity and the essential behavior patterns that make a person different from all others, it is necessary to know who you are.

You know who you are by the way other people treat you. When children are babies, it is their immediate family that helps them shape their identity.

Your parents allow you to do some things, but they make rules about others. They tell you not to hit your brothers and sisters. They tell you to share your toys. If you obey your parents' rules, you will be considered a friendly and generous child.

A child who does not practice self-control and breaks the rules causes turmoil and fights. If you constantly hit your brothers and sisters you will be considered mean. If you don't share your toys, you will be considered selfish.

Your family establishes the rules, but you determine who you will be by how much self-control you use to follow them.

Let's look at Juanita and Manuel, a brother and sister who live in an inner city. Their parents both work. They are not rich, but their basic needs are met.

Juanita is older than Manuel. Their parents ask her to baby-sit with Manuel after school.

"I don't want to take care of Manuel," Juanita whined. "I want to be with my friends."

"You can visit your friends after your mother gets home," Papá said. "If you want nice clothes so you can dress like your friends, your Mamá needs to work. She's not home, so you take care of Manuel."

Juanita threw her books on the table and stomped upstairs, muttering the whole way. "Now I have to call my friends and tell them I won't be able to go shopping with them after school."

"I hate my brother. I hate this family," she complained. "Why couldn't we be rich like Shannon's family. I wish I'd never been born."

All evening Juanita tried to talk her parents out of their decision. Monday arrived, and they still insisted that she watch Manuel.

After school let out, Juanita walked to the elementary school where the sixth-graders were being dismissed. Impatiently she shifted from one foot to the other.

"Where is that dumb brother? He better not be late."

Finally Manuel appeared and came running to her.

"Hi, Sis. It's just you and me today."

"Unfortunately," Juanita muttered. "Let's go."

"How about if we stop at the ice cream store on the way."

"That's not on the way. Besides, you know we aren't supposed to eat sweets before dinner."

"Who's going to know?" Manuel reasoned. "Unless you tell on me."

Juanita stared at her brother and thought about what he had said. After a few seconds she began digging around in her purse and pulled out some coins.

"Here. Take these and go get your ice cream. I'm going over to Lupe's house."

Manuel had reached for the money, but when he heard Juanita's words he lowered his arm.

"You aren't supposed to."

"Who's going to know?" she challenged.

"I'll tell," Manuel said.

"Then I'll tell on you for eating the ice cream."

Manuel thought about it for a minute, then held out his hand. "Okay. I won't tell on you if you won't tell on me."

Juanita gave him the money and watched as he ran to catch up to a friend. He was big for his age and strong. She wouldn't have to worry about him. He was old enough to take care of himself.

Juanita smiled as she hurried toward Lupe's house. She'd

have fun there. Lupe had a great stereo and Juanita loved the posters on Lupe's bedroom wall.

It was close to five o'clock when Juanita rounded the corner into her block. If she hurried she'd be home in plenty of time to clean up any mess Manuel might have made.

She looked up and stopped. Her heart seemed to thud to her toes as she stared at the blinking red lights of the fire truck. Somebody was in trouble. It looked like one of her neighbors . . . Maybe Sra. Garcia.

No, wait. It was *her* house they were at. Oh, no. *Manuel!*

Juanita's parents had an image of Juanita as being the oldest child and responsible. What did she do to that image? Do you think her parents will believe she is responsible now? Why?

In what areas did Juanita lose her self-control? Have you been in similar situations, or do you know of people who are? What effect did her behavior have on the family?

Even if Manuel had taken care of himself for several days, weeks, or months, leaving him alone was an act that could cause potential harm.

Families have rules so that they can function. They need to follow the rules so that they can survive. Small rules may not seem important, but they all add up to a whole.

Let's look at Felicia and Maria. They are neighbors of Juanita, and both sisters go to the high school. Maria has been nominated for Homecoming Queen. Felicia is very happy for her sister.

Felicia was glad school was out. The test in last period was awful. She hoped she had passed it. Before she had gone a block, she heard a shout behind her.

"Sis! Wait up."

Felicia turned and waved at Maria. Her sister's bright smile chased away some of the tiredness she felt.

"What's up?" Felicia asked. "You look all excited."

Maria waved a paper in front of Felicia's face. "It's the schedule for practice and the list of things we have to get."

"What things?" Felicia asked.

"It says here that I need a ball gown for the dance, but I also need a fancy dinner dress. The board takes all the nominees to dinner before the big night."

Felicia's grip on her books tightened. Two dresses? How in the world were Mamá and Papá going to handle that? They had talked until late last night figuring a way to get the ball gown. She had heard them through the thin walls of their bedroom. Maria had been asleep so she didn't know.

"Isn't it the most? Two new dresses." Maria practically skipped along beside her.

Felicia forced a smile. She didn't want to burst Maria's bubble. She would find out soon enough when their parents came home. They would have to tell her.

Felicia walked the rest of the way home deep in thought. Maybe there was a way. As soon as Maria started studying, Felicia began making phone calls. By the time her parents arrived she had good news.

As soon as the car pulled into the driveway, Felicia rushed out and waylaid her parents.

"Before we go in we've got to talk."

"Why? What's the matter?" her mother asked. "Maria is still nominated for Homecoming Queen, isn't she?"

"Sí, mamá." Felicia quickly told them about the dinner.

A frown formed across her father's forehead. Her mother bit her lower lip. "What will we do? We can't afford two dresses."

Her father shifted uncomfortably. "We'll find a way. My baby girl is going to have her moment."

Felicia spoke up. "I called the Community Youth Services. They already have three jobs lined up for me, one baby-sitting and two housecleaning jobs."

"We don't want you working," her mother protested. "What about your studies?"

"It's just until we have enough for Maria's dress," Felicia said. "Maria can help me study."

Both her mother and father gave Felicia a big hug. "You're such a good child. We will make this up to you."

What self-control did Felicia practice? Are there other ways she could have handled the situation? Think about the possibilities and figure out what kind of person would do them.

Felicia is generous and fair and does not harbor jealousy or envy. Maybe she wants a new dress too. Maybe she doesn't really want to do those jobs. Her actions determined her character.

Can you see how self-control brings harmony into the home? Felicia knew that her parents would be worried about the added expense. She prevented that by coming up with a solution. She allowed Maria to remain happy by not telling her about the problem until it had been solved.

Lack of self-control by Juanita created problems. Felicia's self-control solved problems.

Think of your family and list the areas where you show self-control. Study them and see how doing so keeps your family operating smoothly and harmoniously.

Are there areas where you could improve your self-control? Remember the areas involved: morality, honesty, fairness, manners, moderation, forgiveness, generosity, patience, and compassion. If you practice these, your family affairs will run smoothly.

If malicious gossip, anger, jealousy, and envy are not controlled, there will be fights, arguments, and tension.

Think about what kind of family you want to live in. How do you contribute to making it as you desire?

You may think that if you are the only one who does not use obscene language, it won't make a difference. Try it and see what happens. You might find brothers and sisters swearing at each other but not at you.

You control who you are and what part you play within your family.

SELF-CONTROL AT SCHOOL AND WITH PEERS

One of the hardest places to practice self-control is among your peers at school. That stems from the fact that you are

The image you project to your teachers will be different from the one you show your friends.

searching for self-identity and that it involves character and interest.

At school there will be conflicts between these aspects of self-control. Your identity with your teachers is different from that with your peers. If grades and academic success are important to you, you will want to present the image of a studious, hard-working student. To do so, you must control your behavior in a certain manner. For example, you will practice good behavior in class and will not use obscene language. You will do your homework and study for tests.

These things take self-control, because in class with you are your peers. To them you want to appear loose and unconcerned about school. When you hang around with them you might use obscene language because you think it's the accepted behavior. You might be talked into going cruising instead of doing homework.

Others demand another identity from you. Fellow classmates who are not your peers must be considered. If you're a senior you have an image to portray to the younger students. You want to appear confident and "with it." Some teens even display uninterest in anyone younger than they are. This might be counter to your natural generosity or compassion.

Because you need to portray so many identities within the same environment, self-control becomes unstable. Later we will show that you need to set goals and understand established rules to strengthen self-control. That is difficult to do in such a mixed setting.

Jerome and Shawn attend the same high school. Let's see how they handle the conflict.

Jerome cruised into class with his lanky stride. Several girls watched his cool moves, so he continued to slip on by. Out of the corner of his eye he watched Miss Jones. If she saw him acting up, he'd be in trouble. She had made it clear that she wanted students in her class to walk in an orderly fashion to their desks.

Cassandra winked as he approached her desk. He forgot about Miss Jones.

"Jerome Johnson." Miss Jones's deep voice carried across the room. "What do you think you're doing?"

Jerome straightened, but inside he suddenly felt like mush. He glanced at Cassandra. Her brown eyes were wide and questioning. In fact, the whole class was wondering what he would do now.

If he kept cruising he would be "in" with Cassandra but "out" with Miss Jones. Cassandra blinked. Her long lashes shadowed her cheek. When she looked at him with those big brown eyes, he began to *move* down the aisle.

"Jerome, I want to see you after class."

Jerome bit back the protest. It wasn't fair. He was only trying to please Cassandra.

But what about Miss Jones? a voice inside asked.

Jerome squirmed in his chair. He needed a B in English. The only way he could stay on the team was to bring up his grade average. Math was a disaster. English was his only chance.

Jerome didn't hear much of Miss Jones's lecture. He was too busy worrying about what she was going to say after school.

The bell rang, and Jerome's friend Shawn came to the door. "Hey, man. Coach wants us in the gym *now*. Something's come up."

Jerome hurried over to where Shawn stood. Forgotten were Cassandra and Miss Jones.

"What's happening?" he asked.

"Coach got footage of the last game. From what I hear, he's going to chew us out for some big mistakes."

Jerome swore out loud until he realized that Miss Jones was staring at him. A frown creased her forehead, and he knew he had broken another rule.

Too bad. He'd already done it. Might as well be in trouble big since he was already halfway there.

"Look, Miss Jones. We're going to have to talk later. I've got to run."

Can you name all the areas where Jerome failed in self-control? What about the shuffling into class? What code of behavior did he follow and why? What would have happened if he had kept to Miss Jones's standards?

You can see how easily self-control is confused. Jerome was receiving mixed messages within the same environment. If he had been outside, there would be no conflict about the

shuffling. If he had been in the room with only Miss Jones, there would be no conflict about his classroom behavior.

That is what makes self-control difficult in our modern society. It is so complex that people are not sure which codes apply. If they manage to figure that out, they need to decide which ones to follow.

Having your priorities established helps. If you know what kind of person you want to be, you will exert control to project that image.

Let's look at Roshonda and Leanna. They are on the gymnastic team at the club their parents belong to. Roshonda wants to be an Olympic gymnast. She has already set the goal.

Leanna wants to be a gymnast too, but she's not sure she can do it. She thinks Roshonda is much stronger than she.

Conflicts arise. Lets see how the friends manage their self-control.

Roshonda stretched her legs and bent forward. Every muscle screamed with pain. The workout had been strenuous.

Leanna groaned beside her. "I can't believe he made us do those exercises."

"This is only the beginning," Roshonda reminded her. "We have a month of this."

"Does he want to kill us?"

Roshonda chuckled, but she didn't feel all that humorous. "He wants us in shape. These exercises are designed to build up our endurance."

"I don't know about you," Leanna told her, "but I've had it. I'm going to lie around by the pool all weekend and do nothing."

Roshonda thought about the swimming pool in their backyard. Floating in the warm water would be heaven.

"You know what Coach said about keeping toned up over the weekend," Roshonda reminded her friend.

"How's he going to know what we're doing?" Leanna replied. "Besides, I'm paying him to teach me, not the other way around. I should be telling him what to do."

Great self-discipline and sacrifice are required to achieve the goal of an Olympic gymnast.

Roshonda sighed. She had heard that superior attitude of Leanna's so many times she could choke.

"Your folks are paying him good money to teach you. That's reason enough to listen to what he says."

Leanna didn't answer, but pranced off to the showers. Roshonda followed, taking a quick one so she could get home. She was beat. Dinner, an hour of television, and bed; that's what she looked forward to and in that order.

She was blow-drying her hair when Leanna came over to stand by her. "There's a party tonight at Jarad's house. Want to go?"

"You've got to be kidding." Roshonda turned off the dryer. "We have a big day tomorrow."

"I'm tired of all this work and no play. I'm going to the party."

"Don't come crying to me when you can't do your routine tomorrow."

"Don't worry about me," Leanna said as she packed her comb and lipstick into her purse. "I'll see you at ten."

Roshonda shook her head as she put moisturizer on her face. Her skin was beautiful, a rich dark color, and she wanted to keep it smooth. Junk food at the party would ruin that. They would probably be drinking too.

She shuddered as she remembered the one time she had worked out after a late party. It had taken days to get the alcohol out of her system — agonizing days. Her muscles had felt as if weights were attached to them. Leanna would be sorry if she partied tonight.

Roshonda closed her bag and headed out toward her car. The sporty model always sent a thrill through her. Maybe she should go to that party after all. Theo would probably be there.

Thoughts of the brawny senior made her smile. He could melt butter with a look from his dark eyes.

Roshonda paused at the door of the car. Should she go home or to the party?

Their coach walked out of the clubhouse and waved. "See you tomorrow."

Seeing the former Olympic champion reminded Roshonda of her primary goal: Get to the Olympics. She would have her whole life after that to party.

The next day Roshonda was glad of her decision to go home

and to bed. She was getting tired, but her routine was looking good.

Leanna wasn't faring as well. Sweat beaded on her brow and trickled down her back. She wasn't quite in sync. Coach was yelling at her and having a fit.

Roshonda was tempted to say, "I told you so," but decided against it. The poor girl had enough problems without adding to them.

Coach stopped yelling and turned to Roshonda. "Take a break," he told her. "I want to talk to Leanna."

Roshonda left, feeling bad about her friend. Coach would show no mercy, and he was no fool. He would know what she had done.

Leanna was in tears when Roshonda returned. "It's okay, Leanna. He'll get over it." She tried to console her friend. "Come on. I'll help you with this move."

What aspects of self-control did Roshonda show? She reacted to Leanna with compassion. What other ways could she have reacted?

What about Roshonda's decision not to go to the party? Why was Roshonda so self-controlled?

Having set goals makes a difference in how much self-control you exert. Your self-image also has an effect on you. Leanna wanted to be an Olympic star too, but she didn't have the same self-control. Perhaps her desire wasn't as deep as Roshonda's. Maybe her peers exerted pressure that she couldn't hold up against. Remember also that Leanna didn't really believe she was Olympic material.

What you believe about yourself plays an important role in who you are, especially in relation to your peers. Roshonda didn't worry what her friends thought about going to bed early. She was more concerned about her workout the next day. In what other areas did Roshonda show self-control? Can you think of situations with your friends that create conflicts with your self-control? How do you resolve them?

All conflicts can be resolved. A later chapter will go into more detail about attaining self-control. Until then, it is important to believe that your actions and behavior are *yours* to manage.

SELF-CONTROL IN THE COMMUNITY

In today's world self-control is needed in the community and in the workplace. Even though the culture is complex, and even though people may not seem to care because of the large population, your ability to practice self-control is necessary for the survival of the community.

For a complex society to function, everyone needs to do his part. Sometimes an individual does not follow rules or conform. This deviation can be absorbed by the larger group.

For example, if a man loses self-control and starts running wild through the streets, the society has institutions to confine him. If possible, they heal him. If not, they keep him in a hospital where he won't harm himself or others.

Take a criminal as another example. A woman goes into a store and takes what she wants. Envy, greed, sometimes a psychological illness cause shoplifting. All are a result of lack of self-control.

The culture deals with criminals. Just as your parents punished you to teach you to conform to the family code of behavior, the community also establishes punishments. It has law-enforcement officers and courts to carry out the laws and institutions to confine people who break the laws.

Although some lack of self-control can be tolerated, most of the time you are expected to conform to the culture's code of behavior. By doing so, you establish your identity in the community.

A person who steals is a criminal. If you never follow rules you may be considered insane. If you always obey the rules you could be known as a law-abiding citizen. If you volunteer in community services or through your religious organization, you will be considered charitable.

How you act is how you are seen and known. Have you ever been told by your parents not to hang around certain people? That is because they are known for something your parents don't want you to be known for. Their request may seem unfair because you know you are not like that. But your parents know that strangers will associate you with the negative if they see you there.

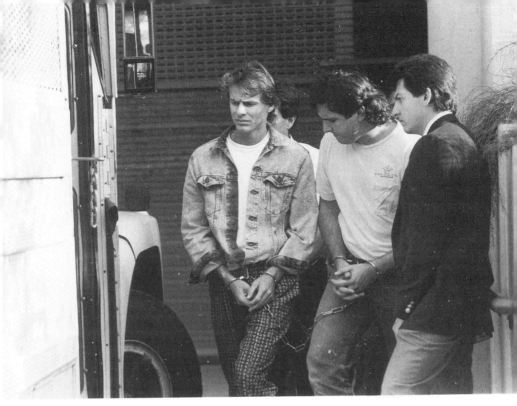

People who break society's laws are punished by the courts.

Let's see how Trevor was identified because of his association with Dave. The boys grew up together as they live only a block apart. Trevor is an honor student, but Dave dropped out of school.

Trevor bounded down the stairs and rushed through the living room into the kitchen. It was Saturday. No school and great weather, it couldn't be more perfect.

In the kitchen he almost ran into his brother, Bob.

"Whoa there! Where's the fire?" Bob teased as he backed up. His blond hair flopped over his eyes.

"No school today," Trevor smiled. "What about you, do you have to study?"

Bob grimaced. "Lab work. I'll be at the university most of the day."

"Tough break," Trevor said as he poured some juice. "You sure do have to study a lot. Maybe I'll change my mind about going to college."

Bob straightened. "Don't you dare! You know Ma wants us to graduate."

"A college degree isn't the only way to get ahead." Trevor popped some bread into the toaster. "Look at Dave. He's a dropout and he makes big bucks."

"Selling drugs, Trev. Don't you even think about doing that."

"No way," Trevor assured him. "Those dudes play rough. I'm too chicken."

"Stay that way." Bob handed him the butter for his toast. "You just keep your mind on college."

Trevor didn't bother to answer. He didn't really mind studying. Besides, he wanted to be just like Bob. His brother was something else.

Trevor put his toast on a paper plate and sat down at the table across from Bob.

"What are you planning to do today?" Bob asked between sips of juice.

Trevor shrugged as he bit into his toast.

"If you feel inspired, you can straighten out the garage."

"Forget that idea," Trevor laughed. "This is my only day off. Maybe I'll go see what Dave's up to. We can go to the park and shoot baskets on the ball courts."

Bob set down his glass with a thud. "Don't go to Dave's."

Trevor stared.

"I mean it, Trev. He's dealing dope. I don't want you associated with him."

"Come off it, Bob. I don't do drugs. Dave knows that. He doesn't even mention them when I'm around."

"Still, you stay clear of him. Ma works hard enough just to support us. She doesn't need the neighbors thinking you're into drugs."

"Who cares about those old gossips?" Trevor said. Annoyance built inside him. He wished Ma and Bob could still like Dave. Sure it was dangerous to deal, but Dave had a new sports car. Ma, Bob, and Trevor were sharing the "old gray goose" they had had since his father died ten years ago.

Trevor knew better than to antagonize Bob. He waited until

Bob was on his way to the university before going down the street to Dave's house. Loud music blasted from the back. Good. Dave was home.

Shortly after Trevor rang the doorbell, Dave greeted him. Dressed in cut-off shorts and a sleeveless shirt, Dave appeared relaxed, but Trevor noticed a worried look in his expression.

"What's the matter?" he asked.

"Nothing." Dave quickly glanced up and down the street before pulling Trevor into the house. "I'm expecting a customer. I thought you were him."

Trevor held his hands out palm up. "No way, man. I'm clean."

Dave slapped Trevor's hands. "When you going to try it? It'll send you flying."

Trevor lowered his hands, and his expression grew serious. "Don't start on me, Dave. I don't want to take that stuff."

Dave's jaw muscle twitched as he clenched his teeth. He stood like that for several seconds until finally he smiled. "Sure, man. Come on out back. I've got a new C.D. Wait 'til you hear it."

Trevor followed his friend, relieved that he hadn't gotten mad. Dave had a temper that was best to stay clear of.

Five minutes later the doorbell rang. Dave tensed. Trevor stared.

"Wait here. That's my man."

Trevor watched Dave pick up a small white packet and stuff it in his pocket. He turned away, wishing he hadn't seen it.

The murmur of voices drifted onto the patio as Dave talked to his customer. Trevor ignored it and listened to the rock band beat out its rhythm.

Suddenly a man charged out the door holding a gun pointed at him. Trevor froze as terror coursed through him. Visions of gang wars clicked as he sat, sweat trickling down his back.

"Stay right there," the man said. "You're under arrest."

To Trevor's astonishment the man flipped out a badge. He sank back in relief. "I'm glad it's you, officer. You scared the . . ."

"Save it," the policeman interrupted. "You've got the right to remain silent . . ."

*   *   *

In what instances did Trevor show self-control? What were the consequences? When did he not show self-control? What happened?

Trevor was innocent, but because he was present during a drug transaction he is considered an accomplice. Not only did his mother's friends think he was into drugs because he associated with Dave, but by his actions he is now under criminal investigation.

Trevor was considered a criminal because of his association with one. Dave was known in the community as one. His actions declared it.

Society makes rules to protect its members. Sometimes we feel frustrated and wonder why we have to follow so many dumb rules. It's because if we don't, we'll have chaos.

What would happen in your community if everyone drove wherever they wanted on the highway instead of staying on their side? Wouldn't it be dangerous to drive? In fact, it is already dangerous to be in a moving vehicle because there are people on the road who do not practice self-control.

If a person drives after drinking alcohol, he is breaking the law, failing to show self-control, and creating a hazard to others.

Running a red light, drag-racing, ignoring road signs, speeding; all of these traffic offenses cause disaster and death every day in American communities.

Can you think of other community laws that require self-control? How do those laws help society? What happens if people don't practice self-control and break the laws?

Another aspect of self-control to consider in today's world is employment. Every job is part of a community within the large society. For example, most businesses have a director, manager, or boss, junior officers, and on down to the bottom of the ladder.

Within each business are company rules. Most of the time those rules coincide with the general society's values. Occasionally they don't. The important thing to remember is that if you wish to stay on that job, you have to practice self-control and obey its rules.

That is why parents, family, teachers, and friends demand that you learn self-control. It is necessary for a culture to remain stable, but it is also important to your own survival.

Will an employer keep someone who is always drunk or doped up? One who is always late or misses a lot of work? Would you want someone working for you who was always getting into fights?

Employers don't want those things. They need order so that they can make a profit. They don't have time to teach you self-control because time is money to them. They have the power to fire you, and if you don't control yourself they will do so.

Let's look at Kathy and Judy. They both have after-school jobs at the local hamburger shop.

Judy flipped over the sizzling beef patties and put the lettuce on the buns, all at the same time.

"Whew, it's busy today," she hollered at Kathy as they finished the last order. "Looks like a break is finally coming up."

"Thank goodness," Kathy said as she plopped packets of mustard and ketchup into the paper sacks.

Out of the corner of her eye Judy noticed that Kathy slipped more packets into her pocket. Strange, she thought and then shrugged it off. Kathy was probably stocking up with extras in case the couple wanted more.

Judy scraped off the grill while Kathy gave the customers their order. The couple didn't ask for more condiments, Judy noticed before she headed for the soda dispenser.

"I'm taking a break," she told Kathy. "Want a soda?"

Manny, their boss, had told them they could have sodas "on the house." He didn't allow them to eat, though; they had to buy their own food. Of course, he gave them a discount.

"Sure, thanks," Kathy said.

Judy turned to fill another glass. As the soda spigot ran, she glanced up and saw Kathy switch the condiments from her pocket to her purse. Not only that, she saw what looked like money.

The soda started overflowing. Judy quickly shut off the

spigot and set the dripping glass on the counter. What should she do? Maybe she should just let it drop. Finally she decided to confront Kathy.

"What are you doing?" she asked.

Kathy stiffened and swung around to face Judy.

"Nothing. Why?"

"Don't lie to me. I saw you put money in your purse. Is it from the register?"

"No big deal." Kathy shrugged and tried to act nonchalant. "It's just a couple of bucks here and there. I do it all the time."

"But what if Manny finds out? You'll be fired. He could even prosecute."

"No way." Kathy swept by her and headed for the cash window. "Manny thinks I'm great, especially after I give him one of my big smiles."

"Does he already know about this?" Judy asked in surprise.

"No. And he won't unless you tell." Kathy punched open the register. "Here, you want some too?"

"He doesn't miss it?"

"Nope. I just don't ring up every sale."

Judy stared. No wonder Kathy was always buying new clothes. It took Judy weeks to save up from just her salary alone.

Kathy held out a couple of dollar bills. "Here, take it. Manny doesn't pay us enough anyway. We deserve it."

For several minutes, Judy debated about taking the money. Finally she pushed Kathy's hand away.

"No. I don't want any part of this," she said, her voice firm and determined.

Think of the self-control Judy used to turn down the easy money. In what other ways did she show self-control?

What about Kathy? Was she exerting self-control? What are the possible consequences of her actions?

We've seen from history the power of self-control. If you examine the world around you, you'll see that you can gain the same control of your life by your own efforts.

How you interact within your family, at school, with friends, and on the job depends upon your decisions and your will.

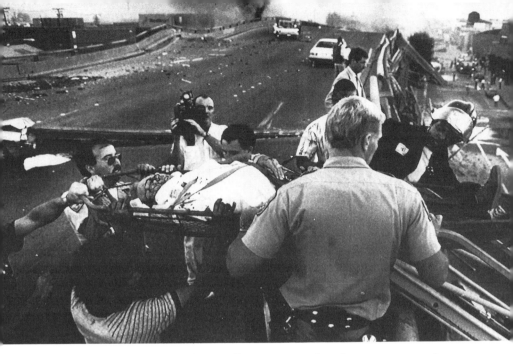

Controlling their own fears, firemen and volunteers work to rescue victims of a devastating earthquake in San Francisco.

Outside circumstances may influence you. Decisions may be tough. You may have help or may have to make choices on your own. These will affect your level of self-control.

It is important, however, to remember that *you* have the say in how you act and how you react. If you care what your community thinks about you, if you are concerned for the welfare of yourself and others, you need to learn self-control.

If your survival is important, you need to examine your place in today's world and see what controls you need to maintain it. If you want to improve your environment or conditions, you must learn to see what is needed, set your goals, and then control your behavior toward that desire.

In the United States today, a person can be and do anything he or she wants. It takes determination and willpower. Astronauts conquer their fears and leave the world they know to explore the unknown. Emergencies occur such as tornadoes, hurricanes, and earthquakes. Under stress people show remarkable self-control and perform acts of heroism.

That self-control is available to everyone. You need only claim it. Remember that self-control involves your character and identity. Determine who you are and then act as if you already are that person. Self-control will make it happen.

CHAPTER 4

Why
Self-control
Is Valued

Self-control is highly valued in most cultures. It is necessary to keep a society functioning, especially one that consists of many individuals. People cannot live, work, or play together unless they exert self-control.

HOW SELF-CONTROL AFFECTS ATTITUDES

Attitude can be a mental position or feeling with regard to an object. It is also the position of something in relation to something else such as a situation or subject.

The latter definition best states how self-control affects your attitudes. People exert self-control because they perceive the need to do so. The need may be simply to avoid punishment or ostracism. Self-control is exerted to accomplish a goal. It can never be forced. You always decide, for your own reasons, that you will control your actions.

How well you control your actions affects your attitudes. If you are successful at following most of the cultural rules, you probably feel good about yourself. A person who performs as expected receives praise, smiles, and encouragement, which contribute to a positive self-image.

A negative self-image forms when you have difficulty exerting self-control. Constant messages from your family, friends, or the community that you are doing wrong will make you feel like a nobody. Depression can result, as well as low self-esteem.

It is easy to blame your environment for these problems. You might say your parents are too strict. Some students say the teachers pick on them. Others feel that they are hassled by their peers.

Most of the time, however, you cannot blame others for your attitude. Your attitude develops out of your own decision to control your actions.

An example would be a student, let's call her Sharon, who gets poor grades in school. Sharon never does her homework, and she fails on tests. Her parents give her a bad time and punish her for every bad grade she brings home.

Sharon hates school. Can you understand why? It is normal to be angry when you fail and when you are punished for that failure. But look deeper into the problem. Why does Sharon fail? Whose decision is it to do homework? Who controls Sharon's behavior? Sharon can be punished and flunked, and neither of those things will make her learn. She has to *want* to learn and then *decide* to control her behavior before she sits down and studies.

When Sharon practices self-control and starts studying, she will be able to change her negative attitude of failure to a positive attitude of success.

Self-control affects all your attitudes. Since self-control determines your identity and character, the way you perceive yourself results in your attitudes. Do you worry about money? What behavior or control on your part will change that attitude of worry? Generosity, moderation, and honesty are some ways. If you worry about money, do you go to the department store and make a purchase on your charge card? That lack of self-control will increase your attitude of worry.

Do you want to have good health? Self-control will benefit your physical condition. Lack of self-control such as overeating, undereating, eating only junk food, not exercising, not dressing for the weather, staying up late — these poor habits create bad health. To correct these habits, *you* have to decide to change your behavior, and that takes self-control.

The attitude of hatred can be changed by controlling jealousy, curbing anger, not giving in to envy. The attitude of selfishness can be changed by practicing compassion, patience, generosity, and forgiveness.

Can you think of other attitudes that can be affected by self-control?

Let's look at Curtis and Troy and see how their self-control affects their attitudes.

Curtis adjusted the volume of his Walkman radio as he walked beside Troy down the busy city street. His favorite song was playing. He shook his head in time to the beat and snapped his fingers.

Curtis was really into the music and didn't see the man until he grabbed Curtis's sleeve.

"Hey!" Curtis swung around and stared at the man.

His shirt was torn and his pants were filthy. His face was stubbled with unwashed whiskers. His eyes were red and desperate. He had probably been sleeping in the alleys.

Repulsed, Curtis jerked his arm away.

The man started talking but Curtis couldn't hear him. He could only see his lips move.

Curtis was glad his radio was too loud. He didn't want to know what the man was saying. With a shrug he turned away. He would have to hurry; Troy was halfway down the block.

"Troy! Wait up," Curtis hollered.

He was about to start jogging when he felt another tug on his sleeve.

"Let go," Curtis said. "I've got to catch up to my friend." This guy was a real pain.

The man spoke again. Curtis tried to pull his arm loose, but the man hung on. Afraid of tearing his shirt, Curtis stopped resisting and turned down his radio.

"Please," the man said. "My family is hungry. I need money for food."

"Forget it," Curtis told him. "If you want money, go get job."

A blank look came into the man's face. His shoulders slumped. For a second Curtis felt pity and almost gave in. Before he could dig into his pocket for some coins, he changed his mind.

"What's up?" Troy suddenly appeared beside him. "One minute we're together and the next thing I know you're not there."

Curtis jerked his thumb toward the man. "He wants money. Says his family needs it. Do you believe the nerve of the guy? He probably wants to buy a bottle of cheap wine."

"No," the man spoke again.

Curtis stared in surprise. Couldn't he take a hint? "Get lost, bozo."

The man cast a pleading glance at Troy. "My family is starving. It's true."

Curtis started to push Troy along. "Come on, man. We don't need this."

"Wait." Troy stepped around Curtis and approached the man. "Where is your family?"

Curtis rolled his eyes. Now what? Troy wasn't going to fall for this gig, was he? Several passers by stared at the odd trio. Curtis shifted restlessly as the man explained that he had left his family at a nearby square.

Troy patted the man's shoulder and said, "Let's go get them. There's a cafeteria nearby. I'll treat you to lunch."

Curtis stared. Troy couldn't be serious — or could he?

As Troy followed the man, he turned to Curtis. "Come on. This ought to be interesting."

Curtis almost refused, but something in Troy's expression of concern changed his mind. Troy was a soft touch sometimes. This creep might be leading his friend into a trap.

The square was two blocks east. Curtis scanned the street carefully as they walked. Once they rounded the corner and crossed into the square, Curtis stared in horror. Men and women were everywhere in the park.

The homeless. He had heard about them on the news, but he hadn't been near them. Everywhere he turned he could see

City dwellers ignore a homeless man as he rummages through a trash can.

ragged clothing and haggard faces. The sight didn't fit — not when he had just left a block filled with smartly dressed business people.

Curtis shifted uncomfortably when the man stopped in front of a bench where a woman and two small children sat. No one else came near them. With disgust he turned away from the vacant stares.

Curtis couldn't describe how he felt when he saw the children's eyes suddenly light up as the man explained Troy's offer. They both stood up. They were rail-thin. Curtis thought they might blow away. They skipped toward Troy and hugged his knees. Suddenly the disgust he had felt disappeared.

It didn't take long to feed the family. Curtis discovered that he could sympathize with the man, who had lost his job and then his house. The man had brought his family to the city, hoping to find work, but all they had found were high prices and more bad times.

The meal cost over thirty dollars — money Troy had saved to buy that new shirt they had seen. Before he realized what he was doing, Curtis took out the twenty-dollar bill he had in his wallet and gave it to the man.

"Here. This might help for tomorrow."

The woman cried and the children laughed. For the first time in ages Curtis felt that he had really done something right. He would probably kick himself later, but for now he felt on top of the world.

When they left the family, Curtis turned to Troy and held out his empty hands. "No sense going shopping now."

"Let's head for home," Troy agreed.

Home. Curtis was suddenly thankful he had one to return to.

What attitude changes did Curtis go through and why? What aspects of self-control changed his way of thinking about the homeless. Think of instances when self-control changed your sentiments.

Curtis's attitude changed from anger and intolerance to compassion. He could have kept his attitude of anger, but what would that do for him? Sure, he would still have his money, but Curtis and Troy had a sense of values, a morality that did not want to see people starve. Their priority became one of compassion and generosity rather than one of selfishness and greed.

The value of this form of self-control is obvious. If people helped each other, we would not have so many hungry and homeless. That would benefit the culture. Remember, for a culture to survive there must be harmony and balance among *all* its members.

Generosity and compassion benefited individuals as well. Obviously the family's needs were met; they received food. Curtis and Troy benefited also. How?

Curtis had been filled with anger and dislike for the beggar. He did not realize the man's true predicament and had formed false judgments. His prejudice prevented him from being generous or compassionate.

Troy, on the other hand, used self-control and withheld

judgment until he had learned all the facts. He was fair and did not listen to Curtis's malicious remarks. With patience and kindness, Troy helped the family and also helped Curtis. By setting an example, he changed Curtis's attitude from a negative one to a positive one.

Negative attitudes are harmful to yourself and to others. Harboring them will eat at your conscience, your health, and your peace of mind. Let's look at Tina and Louisa and see how lack of self-control affects their attitudes and well-being.

Tina sat on the bleachers and tapped her feet to the beat of the music. "I wish these tryouts were over." She leaned toward Louisa and whispered.

"Me, too. Sitting around waiting makes me nervous."

"I want to be cheerleader so bad I can taste it," Tina muttered as she clenched her fists.

"It's not that big a deal, Tina. Just get out there and do your best. It's all you can do."

"What if my best is not good enough?"

"Relax." Louisa took an impatient breath. "We've been practicing all summer. We'll make it."

Tina slipped a stick of gum in her mouth. She had better make it! How else was she going to get someone like Jim to notice her? The star quarterback wouldn't be interested in a nobody like her. She needed the status of the position.

Her glance slid across the football field to where the team was practicing. Jim stood on the sidelines talking to the coach. His blond hair lifted in the breeze. Tina sighed.

Maybe she would have a chance if she were rich or hung around with the crowd that Jim did. But not Tina Rodrigo, whose father was a custodian at the elementary school. She wouldn't interest a guy like Jim on her own merit.

A movement brought her attention back to the foot of the bleachers. The teachers who were to judge the tryouts had finally arrived.

"It's about time," Tina muttered. Bitterness and impatience sounded in her voice. "They couldn't care less about our waiting around and getting more nervous."

"They had classes to teach," Louisa reminded her. "Ease up, girl. You're going to be so nervous you'll flub up."

"Don't even say it," Tina muttered. "This waiting is driving me crazy."

"You can say that again."

Music blared as the first girl began her routine. Tina watched every move. When she saw several mistakes, she relaxed a little. Maybe she had a chance.

By the time twenty girls had tried out, Tina wasn't sure she had a chance at all. Most of the others weren't so hot, but seven she had seen were dynamite. She and Louisa would have to be pretty special to outdo them.

"We're next." Louisa patted Tina's knee.

"I don't know," Tina whispered. "Those last two were so good, and Susie hasn't even done her routine yet."

Louisa's jaw tightened, and Tina knew her friend was losing patience. She clamped her mouth shut and vowed not to say another word. Inside, it felt as if World War III was being fought. Her stomach hurt. Her muscles were stiffening too. *Take a deep breath*, she silently ordered herself.

By the time the last routine was finished, Tina thought she was going to throw up. Louisa stood and Tina got up, too. Her legs felt wobbly, and suddenly she was dizzy. She groped in front of her, trying to see in the darkness enveloping her.

"What's the matter?" Louisa's voice sounded far away, but at least she had grabbed Tina's waist to hold her up.

"You all right?" Louisa asked.

Tina shook her head as she fought off panic. *Don't screw up now.*

"I'm okay." Tina's head was finally clearing. "I was sitting too long. My legs went to sleep on me."

"Maybe we'd better skip a turn . . . "

Tina interrupted. "No. I want to get this over with."

At first Tina did fine, but then she made one small mistake and got so nervous that she ended up making more. Sick at heart, she slumped onto the bench. Her stomach felt on fire. Her world had come to an end. She had blown her chances with Jim.

Tina suffered from jealousy and envy. She wanted Jim's attention, she was jealous of the other contestants, and she envied their prestigious social positions. Tina's lack of self-control in curbing those emotions resulted in twofold harm to her.

Tina allowed her inner tension to build to giant proportions. If she had controlled the envy and jealousy, she might not have been so tense. If she had controlled the tension, she probably would not have blown her routine.

Her failure in the tryout was not the only ill effect of her lack of self-control. What was happening in her body? Do you know the side effects of nervous tension? Ulcers develop, high blood pressure causes dizziness, and some people experience intense headaches or backaches.

Tina's attitude also suffered because of her lack of self-control. Because her envy and jealousy interfered with her performance, she now has lower self-esteem. She has con-firmed her belief that she is not good enough for Jim. She is also bitter.

How could Tina change her behavior and control to benefit rather than harm her? Can you think of instances when you have let tension, envy, or jealousy affect your life? How can you change that?

LACK OF SELF-CONTROL IS DESTRUCTIVE

We have seen how Tina harmed her health as well as her attitude by not controlling her emotions. We can destroy ourselves in many ways, and all of them stem from a lack of self-control.

Some of the destruction is subtle, as in Tina's internal stress. The results of other harmful behavior, such as substance abuse and reckless driving, are more obvious.

It is important to recognize that you are the cause of your own destruction. You are the one who chooses your behavior. You are the one who determines your emotions.

Recognizing this is not always easy. Even with obvious behavior such as substance abuse, you may deceive yourself and say, "This won't harm me." But it does, and in more ways than you might imagine.

Drunk drivers endanger other people's lives as well as their own by their lack of control.

Alcohol, for example, is addictive. Some people have a high tolerance for it and do not become addicted until after years of use and abuse. A friend of yours may drink every day and brag about how he or she can stop anytime. He or she may even go a week without drinking to prove it.

However, alcohol abuse has more side effects than addiction. Alcohol is a depressant. Continued use can cause depression and paranoia. Maybe you have noticed that this person no longer seems friendly. A long-term drinker becomes antisocial, angry at the world, and sinks into chronic depression. This substance abuse prevents compassion, fairness, patience, manners. Have you ever seen a polite drunk?

Not only are substance abusers destroying themselves, but they lack judgment and self-control. They do not follow rules. That makes them a hazard to others. In the United States and many other countries, drunk drivers are the cause of many deaths and injuries on the roads and highways.

Heavy drinkers and drug abusers become violent and abusive. They often lose control of their emotions such as anger, jealousy, hatred, and envy. That makes them unpleasant to be around and potentially dangerous.

People who use alcohol or drugs cannot blame the destruction on anyone but themselves. Outside circumstances may contribute to it, but the ultimate decision to use self-control is yours. The obvious result of substance abuse is that instead of your controlling it, the substance controls you. Total lack of control is demeaning and leads to death.

Sexual indulgence is another part of teen life that can come to control you rather than your controlling it. Charlene found out the hard way what damage she could do by failing to control her behavior.

The city lights sparkled in the distance, but it was dark at the top of the hill where Brent had parked the car. The only light was the dim glow from the dashboard clock and radio. Charlene curved closer to Brent, enjoying the cozy atmosphere.

Brent draped his arm across her shoulders and pulled her into his lap. "Comfy?" he asked, his smile devastating as usual.

Charlene reached up and put the tip of a finger in the dimple that creased his cheek.

He grabbed her wrist and began kissing the sensitive skin. Charlene's breath caught.

"You smell good," Brent murmured. "I love your perfume." He leaned forward and nuzzled the cascade of hair that flowed into her neck. "And I love your hair."

Did he love her? she wondered. He had never come right out and said so. But if he loved everything about her, wouldn't it follow that he loved *her*?

Brent's hand slid down her back. She could feel his fingers slip beneath the waistband of her slacks. Charlene tensed, wanting what was happening, yet afraid too.

"I want you, Charlene," Brent whispered before he kissed her. "We're alone. Now's our chance."

Charlene let the pleasure of his kiss wash through her, but

her mind raced. She knew very well what Brent wanted. She also knew that if he didn't get it he would dump her for someone else. Her friend Carol had dated him last year. Carol knew all about it.

Charlene broke the kiss and leaned back against the steering wheel. Brent's face was faintly lit up by the glow of the city lights. The shadows made him look sexy and appealing. She reached up to stroke his chin.

Brent smiled. "You want it too, don't you?"

Charlene hesitated. She could get pregnant, and what about all the diseases she had heard about in school? Did Brent have any protection, she wondered. She was too embarrassed to ask.

"I want you to love me," she whispered, hoping he would say the words. If he loved her he would take care of her if anything happened — like pregnancy.

"We'll make love. Now." He leaned forward and kissed her again.

It wasn't exactly a commitment, but it was close. Charlene closed her eyes, wondering what to do.

Often while dating the question of sex becomes an issue. What self-control does Charlene need to employ? What does she need to consider?

Charlene is no fool. She is aware of the dangers of intercourse, and she is aware that pregnancy can occur. If she is aware of these things, whose responsibility is it to control the situation?

Sexually transmitted diseases are deadly. Venereal diseases can make you sterile and can cause insanity. AIDS causes death.

Charlene has to be a strong person and full of confidence to control her physical desires. She likes Brent and is attracted to him. It is natural for her to want to make love with him. But the consequences *must* be weighed.

Charlene needs to know who she is. If she is confident enough to withstand a rejection from Brent, she might decide not to take the risk involved. However, if she is insecure and her attitude about herself is poor, she may feel that she needs Brent's approval. To a person who does not think highly of herself the popularity would be more important than the risk.

Another consideration is her goals. If Charlene wants to be a teacher and knows she has to go to college, the possibility of pregnancy would limit her options. Many districts will not hire a mother of illegitimate children, on grounds that she will set a bad example for students. Do you think Charlene would risk pregnancy if that were her goal?

If Charlene does not have a particular goal, pregnancy might not seem such a threat. In fact, she might welcome a baby. It could be someone to love.

Sometimes when you don't feel loved or needed, you lower your self-esteem and allow things to happen to you. You lose self-control because you feel you don't deserve any better. That attitude needs to be changed, because it leads down a perilous path.

If you cannot say no to alcohol, drugs, or sexual indulgence you need to examine your goals and your self-image. Counselors at school and religious centers can help you. Large communities have crisis centers and services for guidance.

Learning to say no strengthens your self-control. The stronger you become, the healthier you will be. Every time you don't say no, you weaken your ability to control your behavior. Thoughts creep in — "I'm so awful," "I drank too much last night," "I shouldn't have gone out with Brent."

Guilt can destroy you as much as the act itself. Every time you do something wrong and let guilt take over, it lowers your self-esteem and your desire to maintain control.

Let's look at Alaina and Carolyn. Both girls have a weight problem and want to lose excess pounds. Let's see how attitude works with self-control to produce results.

"Look at those chocolates." Alaina nudged Carolyn and pointed to the display across the mall.

"Who needs to look?" Carolyn sniffed. "I can smell them a mile away."

Alaina chuckled. "Let's go by quickly. If we keep looking, you know we'll be over there buying."

Carolyn kept up as Alaina hurried down another corridor of the huge mall. Her stomach growled in protest. What she'd give for just one bite!

"Look at those dresses." Alaina stopped in front of a popular boutique. "Can't you just picture us in those?"

"No way," Carolyn protested. "We'd look like two whales stuffed in a sardine wrapper."

"That's a poor attitude," Alaina pouted. "You have to believe you're going to be able to wear them."

Carolyn shrugged. "Even if I were thin enough to wear that, can you see me in it? No way. I'd be a geek dressed all hip."

Alaina shook her head. "Not me. If I were that thin I *would* be hip."

"You don't get all shy and embarrassed the way I do," Carolyn reminded her. "I've seen you get out and dance even when you look like this."

"I'm not going to stop living because I'm fat." Alaina propped her hand on her hip. "What's wrong with you today? You sound depressed."

"I am," Carolyn agreed. "I'm tired of being fat, and I hate having to diet all the time."

"I get tired of it too," Alaina agreed, "but I'm determined to get it off this time. I can do it. I know I can."

"Well, I can't." Carolyn swung around. "I'm going back there and get some chocolate."

"No, wait!" Alaina hurried after her. "Let's think about it some more. Talk to me."

"There's nothing to talk about. I've had it."

"Come on, Carolyn. Give it another chance."

Carolyn halted her long strides and turned to face Alaina. Tears brimmed in her eyes. "It's no use. I'll never be thin. I hate myself. Even if I were thin I'd still be ugly. The only thing that will make me happy is candy."

With that she hurried down the mall toward the candy store. Alaina watched her go, saddened by her friend's unhappiness. Alaina wanted to be thin, but she didn't think she was ugly because of her weight. Besides, by summer she would have it off. She already had a fluorescent orange bikini picked out to wear.

In his determination, Walter Hudson has dieted his way to 562 pounds from an original weight of over 1000 pounds.

Can you see how Alaina's positive self-image enabled her to practice her self-control. She had a goal also. In fact, Alaina was visualizing herself as already thin. That is an important process in changing poor habits. See yourself as already where you want to be.

Remember that self-control is self-identity. Alaina knew who she was, and she controlled her behavior to fit the visual image of herself.

Carolyn, on the other hand, believed she was ugly and worthless. If you feel that way about yourself, is there much incentive to be controlled? Carolyn figured, "What the heck," she was already fat; why not have her chocolate?

People use the same destructive rationalizing for drugs, alcohol, cigarettes, and other abusive indulgences.

The key to successful self-control is to set goals and believe that you can accomplish them. Trust in your own ingenuity to solve the problems that come up along the way, and act as if you already are who you want to be.

HOW SELF-CONTROL ENRICHES YOUR LIFE

It doesn't take much digging in the memory bank to recall friends or relatives who generally practiced self-control. Some of the people you have known, however, lacked control in certain areas. Maybe they were selfish or dishonest but were never angry or jealous. Some of your acquaintances may have been lacking in several of the aspects of self-control.

No one has perfect self-control. For one thing, what is perfect to you may not be perfect to your friends. It is relative.

Second, it is human not to be perfect. Too many pressures tug on us to make that possible. Complex societies create even more difficulties, since you are expected to have different degrees of control for each subculture or environment.

Once you realize that you don't need to be perfect, you can unload that pressure from your mind. The next thing to do is decide, in order of preference, the areas you need to work on. Even if you concentrate on only one at a time, you will notice an improvement in your attitude and overall life-style.

For example, if Greg plays golf and likes to win a round with his friends, it is very easy and therefore tempting to fudge on his score. No one will notice if he kicks the ball out of the gopher hole. Who's going to remember exactly how many shots he took on that long green?

What if Greg decides to work on honesty for a change? What if he decides to play by the rules for a month and manages the self-control to do so? How do you think he will feel?

If he fails he will be disappointed, but he could succeed. How do you think he feels about himself deep inside if he wins by cheating? If he wins by using self-control and obtaining his score fairly? His confidence and self-image will surely rise several notches.

Managing to control your behavior produces positive rewards from those around you. Those reinforcements build your self-image. If people around you seem to think you're great, you must believe you are.

Wouldn't you rather have people think good things about you? Everyone likes to be treated with respect. What most people don't realize is that the way people treat you depends upon you.

It's easy to blame others for ill treatment. You can say that you are full of anger because you've been abused by your parents. You may be envious because you are poor. But those negative attitudes can be changed.

A person can control the anger and by doing so, nullify the ill effects of abuse. A person can control the jealousy and envy, leaving room for the creativity and growth needed to climb out of poverty.

Let's look at Tasha and Rose and see how controlling their thinking and behavior enriched their lives.

"I hate geometry," Tasha muttered. "Ms. Calgon always makes me feel like a dummy."

"How's that?" Rose asked as she stuffed her book into the locker.

"She gets so mad when I don't do the problems right."

"Have you talked to her after school?" Rose asked. "Have you explained that you don't understand?"

"Yes, and that's when she acts so mean."

"Maybe she's tired. Why not try before school?"

"That's not it. I think she hates me 'cause I'm black."

Rose slammed her locker shut and stared. "Get serious! Why would she teach here? The whole student body is black."

"Don't be naive." Tasha pulled a sweater out of her locker and slipped it on. "Just because she's here doesn't mean she likes us."

"I think you're exaggerating," Rose said. "There could be lots of reasons she gets impatient."

Tasha grabbed her books and closed her locker. "Like what? She eats nails for breakfast?"

Rose laughed as she followed Tasha down the hall. Tasha passed by Room 411 and looked in to see Ms. Calgon standing behind her desk. She could feel hatred building as she looked at the stringy straight hair and haggard features of the teacher.

"I try so hard," Tasha said. "She never smiles at anyone, even the students who do well in class."

"Sounds to me like she might have some problems. Maybe she needs a little sunshine in her life." Rose sidestepped past two senior basketball players.

Tasha took one look at them and forgot about Ms. Calgon until Rose tugged on her sleeve.

"Pay attention. You're going to make a fool of yourself staring like that."

Tasha grinned. "I know, but whenever I look at Jeff I get all weak in the knees."

"Heaven help us," Rose lifted her hands in mock despair.

"Speaking of help, what am I going to do about Ms. Calgon?"

Rose took a few steps, her expression faraway as if she were deep in thought.

"I know!" Tasha had an idea. "How about getting transferred into another class. Who needs geometry anyway?"

"You do," Rose reminded her. "You want to go to college, remember?"

Tasha groaned.

"Running away from a situation never solves anything. You're always going to run into people like Ms. Calgon."

"That's such a comfort. Thanks a lot," Tasha commented wryly.

"Look, my grandmother had a solution to this problem. It sounds kind of crazy, but I've tried it and it worked for me."

"I'll try anything," Tasha told her friend.

"Now, don't laugh; you have to be serious about this or it won't work."

Tasha was becoming curious, mainly because Rose was getting so nervous. "Okay. I promise."

"Whenever you're around Ms. Calgon, look at her and say to yourself, 'I love you.' "

Tasha halted in mid-stride. "You're right. It's crazy."

"I told you it sounds strange, but hear me out."

Tasha frowned as disappointment grew. She had hoped Rose could really help.

"Don't say it out loud. You don't have to like what she does, but surround her with positive thoughts. My grandmother calls them love darts."

To Tasha's surprise, she realized that she was indeed considering Rose's bizarre idea. What did she have to lose? The situation was getting critical.

"I don't know if I can really say anything about love, even in my thoughts," Tasha said.

"Just give it a week and see what happens."

Tasha decided to go ahead and try it, but she had serious doubts. A week later she searched the hall for Rose during the lunch break. When she found her she pulled her aside.

"Wait till you hear what's happened," Tasha excitedly told her friend.

"You're going out with Jeff?" Rose smiled.

"No, silly. I tried what you said. You know, the 'love darts'. You won't believe what happened!"

Rose's smile deepened. "I bet I can guess."

Tasha didn't wait for her to do so. "I can't believe the change in Ms. Calgon."

"She actually smiled?" Rose asked.

"Well, not that dramatic," Tasha said, "But she hasn't hassled me once all week. Today in class she even praised me for solving a problem."

"See? It works."

Tasha stopped and looked at Rose. A frown chased her happy expression away. "But how does it work? I don't understand why saying something just in my head can make her change."

"It's not the fact of saying words," Rose explained. "It's your attitude that changes. It is hard to react defensively to Ms. Calgon when you're sending 'love darts'. Because you don't react, she doesn't react."

Tasha shook her head, still not sure she understood.

"You don't know what Ms. Calgon's life is like. Maybe she has a lot of problems. Maybe she gets nervous around all of us. It was probably a nice relief to her that you weren't reacting so negatively in class."

"Well, I don't understand, but I'm sure not complaining if it keeps her happy and off my back."

They started on down the hall when Jeff and a friend walked by. A mischievous twinkle sparkled in her eye as she wondered if those 'love darts' would work on him.

To her surprise, Jeff looked directly at her and smiled.

Learning to control our negative reactions will keep the negative forces from influencing our life. Conversely, learning to focus on positive reactions will bring in the positive forces.

How you control your behavior determines what your quality of life will be. An angry, jealous person attracts negative feelings from others. A compassionate, forgiving person invites friendly behavior.

Think about the people you like and love. What qualities make you feel that way about them? What self-control do they exhibit in their lives?

When you are close to people and you know that they are exerting self-control to overcome problems, it makes you really appreciate them. Everyone has problems and attempts to control them in some way. Even Ms. Calgon had to be experiencing them. If you offer positive forces, they will help everyone you meet to deal with their efforts at self-control.

It is easier to keep envy and jealousy from growing if you are around generous people. It is natural to be fair when you are around honest people. Gossip becomes a pleasure when it is nice things you're saying about others.

Problems will always confront you. That is a fact of life. The question is whether you are going to let them control you or you are going to maintan self-control and overcome them? Some problems won't be overcome, but you need to press onward and struggle *through* them.

Often people get bogged down with problems and negative feelings because they focus all their thoughts and energies on the actual problems. That is a dangerous practice because the problems start to appear overwhelming. When that happens, you start believing that you can't control them, which tempts you to give up and not practice your self-control.

Those who see their problems as a challenge and continue to focus on the positive things going on in their life, strengthen their confidence. A good self-image is a result of self-control.

You can decide which of these conditions you want for your life. You can determine the state of your well-being. By focusing on the good things around you and by practicing the elements of self-control such as generosity, fairness, honesty, compassion, morality, and forgiveness, you can live a rich life full of happiness and well-being.

CHAPTER 5

How to Develop Self-control

Human beings have an innate sense for self-control. Often called our sixth sense, it is programmed into our system for survival. For example, if you touch a hot stove and burn your hand, you learn to control your urge to touch another hot stove. An inner voice warns you, "Do not touch."

Experience teaches you how to control your behavior. If you hit your older brother and he hits you back, you learn to control your urge to hit your brother. If you smile at your mother and she smiles and says "I love you," you learn to be generous with your expressions.

These manners and morals are taught from infancy and become innate. They become your nature. You respond automatically.

Some innate controls exist within you from birth. Intuition is a strong voice for self-control. Unfortunately, few people listen to it as much as they should. Let's define it and see how you can strengthen it in your life to give you more self-control.

Intuition is the power or faculty of knowing things without conscious reasoning. It is quick and ready insight. Have you ever been on your way somewhere when something, a hunch, said go another way instead of by your usual route? Or have you started to say something to a friend and a voice inside told you not to say it because it would hurt that person? That is intuition.

It is your innate warning system to practice self-control. It is often a response to thought waves generated around you, which are not at a conscious level but still do affect you. For example, have you ever met a stranger and had an inner feeling tell you not to talk to him or her? Perhaps that person is thinking negative or malicious thoughts about you or has evil intentions. Your intuition picks up the mental messages and warns you, giving you a premonition of danger.

You may think some people are born with more intuition than you. That is not true. Those people have simply developed their intuitive power. You can strengthen yours. It takes patience and practice, but once learned it can be a powerful tool for self-control.

The problem most people have is that they react before listening to what their intuition tells them. For example, if you are heading for the checkout line at the grocery store and someone shoves in ahead of you, your immediate reaction is to strike out at that person. You may want to shove back or swear or yell.

However, if you wait and open your mind to your sixth sense, you might perceive that the person is very upset or perhaps ill. By using your intuition, you might feel compassion. By patiently smiling and forgiving the rude behavior, you practice self-control. You may also give the frustrated person a boost of positive thinking to brighten his or her day.

Can you see how intuition can enable you to practice self-control? What did you and the frustrated shopper gain from polite manners and a smile? If you had become angry before listening to your intuition, what would be the reactions of you and the shopper? Which do you prefer?

Most of you have probably heard parents, teachers, and others tell you to think before you speak. By doing so, you give yourself a chance to listen to your intuition. It sounds like an idealistic practice, but it is just as real as using your other five senses.

Would you walk into a room with your eyes closed? You would want to see where you were going. You use your sense

We should "listen" to feelings that may warn of danger.

of sight to guide you so that you do not run into furniture or people.

If you smell smoke, don't you "listen" to that sensory warning and investigate? You check to see what is burning and whether you need to do something about it. You use your sense of smell.

When you hear a baby cry or a shout of warning, you respond to the sense of hearing by rushing to help or to comfort. Sounds warn you of danger as well: a car honking, a train whistle down the tracks, an animal's growl. You listen to this sense and determine your behavior.

Taste is another sense that you pay attention to. For example, if you eat something moldy your sense of taste warns you that the food may be spoiled. You "listen" to this sense for your protection.

The fifth sense, that of touch, is also important to survival. You can feel if the water is too cold to swim in. You can feel the cold wind on your skin and know that you need to put on a jacket. By listening to the messages of touch, you decide your behavior.

It is commonplace to follow the common-sense messages from your five senses. Your sixth sense or intuition is just as important for your survival. Stop and "listen" to your hunches, your inspirations, and your perceptions just as you rely on the other senses.

If you have a hunch to go to the movie instead of the ball game, follow it. If you don't know whether or not to buy a new dress, pause for a few minutes and listen to your intuition. When interacting with others, be patient and wait before you react to their words or actions. Let your perception give you compassion, patience, and moderation.

Let's see how Tony and Dominic react to intuition.

Dominic paused at the edge of the ridge and peered down the wooded hill. "Have you ever seen such perfect ski conditions?" he asked as he gestured toward the steep incline.

Tony's skis swished through the new-fallen snow as he came up beside Dominic. "Great powder," he agreed.

Dominic stood for several minutes admiring the spectacular view. Tony didn't seem to mind the pause, and Dominic was glad. He never got enough of looking across the snow-covered peaks. Standing at the top of a mountain always gave him a sense of power as well as peace.

"Which way are we headed?" Tony broke the silence with his question.

Dominic glanced to his right. The slope was steeper there. "That's the advanced trail. Killer Hill. It's dangerous and fast."

"Sounds good," Tony assured him. "I can do it. Piece of cake."

Dominic pointed to the left. The trail wound through the trees at a more leisurely pace. "That trail isn't as much of a rush, but it's where most of the girls ski."

Tony had already pointed his skis toward the fast trail, but now he paused to reconsider. Dominic chuckled, knowing the choice between speed and the opposite sex would be difficult for his friend. Dominic had no problem: He was going to go for speed. Candy wasn't skiing today, and she was the only female he was interested in.

Dominic waited while Tony thought about his options. Suddenly a chill traced down his spine. He stared down the steep slope of Killer Hill, trying to shake the premonition of danger.

Tony interrupted his thoughts. "What the heck. Let's go for it. We can catch the women tonight at the club."

Tony started to edge toward Killer Hill, but Dominic grabbed his arm and stopped him. "No. Wait. Let's go the other way."

"I thought Candy was at the homecoming committee meeting."

"She is, " Dominic agreed.

"Then why do you want to go that way?"

Good question, he thought. He couldn't say exactly. He just knew he wasn't going to go down the steep trail.

"Trust me on this," Dominic told his friend.

"What's the matter? Going chicken on me?" Tony laughed as he made clucking noises.

"I've skied this trail dozens of times. Get real." Dominic sounded confident, but in a way Tony was right. He sensed that something was wrong on that trail. His instincts were usually pretty sharp.

Just then two skiers passed by on their way down the easier trail. Dominic seized the opportunity to convince Tony. "Did you see those snow bunnies?"

Tony whistled as he caught sight of the attractive girls.

"Let's go get 'em," Dominic yelled as he pushed off through the trees.

As soon as he headed down the trail he felt a profound sense of relief. He knew he had made the right choice, but he still wondered why he had felt so strongly about Killer Hill.

At the bottom of the hill they headed for the lift for another ride up to the top. As they waited in line, a conversation captured their attention.

"It was awful. They were going so fast they couldn't stop."

"Everyone was piling up."

"Two guys broke their legs."

"I heard it was three."

Dominic interrupted. "What happened? What are you talking about?"

One of the skiers ahead of them turned and said, "Killer Hill.

Two guys collided right under the jump. Everyone behind them couldn't stop and crashed on top of them."

Dominic paled. Tony stared, and he could read the same measure of horror and relief that he felt. "It's a good thing we didn't go down that trail."

Dominic agreed, glad he had listened to his intuition.

Psychologists are proving that premonitions are the work of our sixth sense, which picks up the thought waves of danger. Dominic trusted his inner voice and listened, saving his friend and himself from a possible accident.

Because he recognized what had warned him, he trusted his instincts. He was lucky to find out what had happened. The knowledge made him believe in his power to perceive danger.

Sometimes we never know why we get the feelings we do. Because of that we don't always listen to our sixth sense. We don't believe in it.

Have you ever had a hunch not to do something and after you've gone ahead and done it you said, "I wish I hadn't done that. I knew better, but . . . " Most of us have had that experience. It goes away if you train yourself to listen.

Did you notice that Dominic had paused at the top of the hill? If he had skied off the lift and charged right down Killer Hill, he wouldn't have felt the premonition of danger.

It is important to take a few seconds before making any major choice and listen to all your senses. These provide your innate ability for self-control.

Stopping to think about actions and reactions is difficult to do. Often our instincts war with each other. Let's see how that happens with Carmen, Tanya, and Angela.

The volleyball sailed high into the air and came down to her right. Carmen quickly stepped over and tapped the ball up and to Angela. It was a perfect setup. Angela jumped in the air and spiked the ball into the opposite court. Everyone cheered.

"All right, Angela!"

"Good shot."

Carmen sighed. Angela got the credit, but she had set the ball up for her. Why didn't she get any appreciation? Tanya came up and put an arm across her shoulders.

"Nice setup." She smiled at Carmen.

Carmen stood still, surprised and delighted. "Thanks, Tanya. I'm glad someone appreciates what I do."

Tanya's smile disappeared, and a sad expression crossed her face. "I know what you mean," she said.

Carmen stared, aware that Tanya had meant much more than she had said. Everyone knew that Tanya was one of their best players. They all told her many times how great she was. So what was she talking about? Who didn't appreciate her?

There was no time to ask. Angela was getting ready to serve. Carmen quickly focused her attention back on the game.

They made three more points and won the game. Now it was one to one. Their team had to win this match to tie for the championship. Luckily they had a time-out break.

In the locker room Carmen saw Tanya standing alone. She left Angela and the others and took Tanya a piece of ice.

"Here, this will cool you down."

"Thanks." Tanya smiled, but Carmen had seen the sad look in her eyes.

"What's the matter?" Carmen asked. "You seem down."

"I'm playing my share." Tanya was quick to defend herself. "I made most of those points."

"No, no," Carmen hurried to explain. "It wasn't that. I just mean that every once in awhile you look sad."

Tanya gripped the door of her locker and sighed. "Does it show that much?"

Carmen shrugged. "Only to me. I guess I've always been kind of sensitive."

Tanya blinked a couple of times, and Carmen suddenly had the feeling she was fighting back tears. Carmen wanted to put her arms around Tanya but knew that would really be weird. When Tanya didn't say anything, Carmen figured maybe she wanted to be left alone. Reluctantly she joined Angela and the others.

The last game was tough. The other team kept gaining points on them. Tanya, Angela, and Carmen fought to keep up. Every time the others made a point, Carmen's team made one, but they couldn't get ahead.

Finally it was near the end. The score was tied. Carmen's team had to make two points to win. Thankfully it was Tanya's serve.

Tanya stepped back and served the ball over the net. It sailed by fast and hard, but the other team returned it. After several volleys, they gained the point.

Tension crackled across the court as they waited for Tanya to serve the last ball. If they made this point they'd go to the finals.

Tanya served, but the ball was low and plowed into the net. Angela turned and yelled. "Now's a fine time to screw up. What were you thinking of?"

Carmen gasped and then quickly ran to Tanya. "It's all right. We'll get the ball back."

But it wasn't all right. The opposing team served the ball right at Tanya, but she was so upset that she missed the return.

Again Angela yelled.

Carmen hurried over to Angela. "You're making it worse by yelling. Just calm down and watch your own playing."

Angela bristled with frustrated anger. The ball was served, and this time it was Angela who missed. Everyone groaned. They had lost their chance for the championship.

Several incidents in this scene showed self-control. Can you identify them? Carmen made a great setup in the beginning. How did Angela react, and how did Tanya react? What were the effects of those two different reactions on Carmen's playing?

Tanya showed compassion. Do you think that made Carmen more inclined to care about Tanya's problems? Carmen sensed that something was upsetting Tanya. Maybe she had had a fight with her boyfriend, or maybe someone in her family was sick or in trouble. It doesn't matter whether you know what the problem is. What is important is to sense it and then use self-control in reacting to it.

Angela did not sense Tanya's problem. Her full attention was on winning the game. But did she help her team's cause when she became impatient with Carmen and Tanya? Angela did not forgive their mistakes, nor did she show any compassion or understanding that something might be upsetting their star player. Perhaps if she had, she could have changed her tone, controlled her negative reaction, and made it easier for her team.

Have you been in situations where people have been short-tempered with you? How do you react? What kind of behavior will help the situation, and how does that work?

Your innate sense of control helps you to function in society. Family also plays a big role in developing your self-control. Your family is the first community that you must function in. You have to learn to get along in order to survive.

Your parents and older brothers and sisters work to shape your behavior so that you will conform to their way of doing things. They do so to keep the group in harmony. If members do not follow the set pattern of behavior the situation becomes very uncomfortable and tense.

At the beginning of this chapter we mentioned that you learned not to touch a hot stove because the first time you did you burned your hand. Families use the same technique to socialize you.

If you hit your brothers and sisters you are punished. If you start to run into the street, your mother scolds you and punishes you again. Babies learning to crawl who head for the stairs are restrained. Pretty soon you learn to control your behavior, to do what your family wants so that you won't be punished.

Is this punishment cruel? Usually it is for your protection and safety. Parents and other family members punish because they love you. They want you to learn to control your behavior because they care about your survival.

Some family members lack self-control themselves, and punishment can become abuse. Observe carefully the reasons why your family punishes you. If it's done out of love, you need to take steps to learn control. If it is abusive, you can take steps to get help. Religious organizations, schools, and community organizations offer services to protect you against abuse.

If, however, you use your innate perceptions and see that self-control is basically for your benefit, you need to be the one to start controlling your behavior. By the time you are a teenager, your parents and family should not need to exert measures to control you. By that age you are capable of controlling yourself.

When you show your family that you can maintain self-control, trust develops and you are given more responsibility. Show self-control and your family will give you the freedom to exert your own control.

If, on the other hand, you cannot show self-control, your family will try to control your behavior. They will make strict rules and probably punish uncontrolled behavior. They do this because they care.

Josh and Aaron are brothers. Watch how they strengthen their self-control.

The desert air was dry and the sun hot on his back as Josh paused outside the gate and waited for his brother to drive the pickup truck off the highway. It rattled across the cattle guard and pulled to a stop on the government property. Josh pulled on the barbed wire and closed the gate.

Excitement coursed through him. He and Aaron had planned this trip all week. They were going to cross seventy miles of rugged desert. They had spent all their time after school getting their Honda dirt bikes tuned up. Today was their chance to ride.

Josh hopped in the truck and gave the thumbs-up sign to Aaron. His older brother smiled and put the vehicle in gear. Dust clouded behind them as they bounced along the dirt road. A jackrabbit bounded across in front of them. A hawk soared in the clear morning air.

"Did you remember the repair kit?" Aaron asked.

"You bet. I didn't forget anything." He wouldn't dare. This was the first time Aaron had invited him to join his friends when they went cross-country trail riding. No way was he going to blow it by forgetting something. "I even have the first-aid kit Mom insisted on."

Aaron laughed, and Josh joined him. They both suffered through their mother's overprotectiveness.

Josh saw the other pickups before Aaron did. "Some of the guys are already here."

Aaron swerved off the road into the clearing where the other trucks were parked and honked the horn. Everyone waved and hollered a welcome. Josh watched Aaron carefully and tried to do evrything he did. He felt like jumping out of the truck and skipping around, but that would be totally uncool. He stretched as Aaron did and casually strolled over to the group gathered around a brand-new motorcycle.

The bike was neat, but Josh didn't pay it that much attention. He was too busy checking out Aaron's friends. They wore bright fluorescent biker shirts covered with logos. Helmets, gloves, and gear lay about. Ice chests were full of drinks. Two of the guys had on kidney belts, and Josh wondered if he would need one. The ride in the truck had been jolting. The desert roads were rutted and full of potholes.

"How far we going?" Aaron asked his friends.

"Out to Coyote Springs and then around Table Mountain."

"Your brother going to be able to make it?"

Josh stiffened, aware that he was a newcomer and younger. Aaron shifted uneasily, and for a second Josh wondered if his brother was sorry he had brought him along. Then Aaron's face split into a grin. "He'll outride you, Bernstein."

Josh relaxed when the others started laughing. After that, they talked more about their bikes, and Josh began to worry. What if he couldn't keep up? What if he let his brother down? He'd die first, he decided.

It took another hour before everyone was finally ready to ride. Josh revved up his engine and fought the urge to tear out ahead of everyone. If he took off now, he could show them how well he could ride. Heck, he could pop a wheely right here and scream his engine until he was flying.

Aaron must have read his mind, because suddenly he rolled up beside him. "You stay behind me, you hear?"

"I was going to wait for you up at that wash."

"No stunts, Josh. No showing off. It's dangerous, and we're too far out in the boonies."

"But . . . " Josh started to protest.

"I mean it. You follow and do everything I do, or you don't go."

Rebellion flared in Josh. His brother had no right treating him like a kid, especially in front of his friends. For a second he thought about riding out, but when he saw the worry in his brother's eyes he eased up on the throttle.

Aaron had done him a favor by bringing him out here. He didn't need any flak. Besides, if Josh gave Aaron trouble, he wouldn't bring him again.

"Lead on. I'll eat dust today, but you watch. It won't be for long."

Relief showed in Aaron's face as he snapped his helmet into place. Josh checked to make sure all his straps were secure before he followed his brother's lead.

In how many ways did Aaron and Josh practice self-control? Was Aaron generous and compassionate? What did he demand of Josh? Was it fair?

Josh could have done many things to step out on his own and prove his individuality. He didn't. Instead he yielded to his older brother's demands. Why?

Can you think of instances when family members demanded that you practice self-control? Wasn't it for your own protection?

When you love or care about others, you set rules and standards for them to follow. This is to teach self-control. So if you want to *learn* self-control, it is a wise practice to observe and follow those you admire.

Josh thinks Aaron is great. Aaron is indeed popular and has many friends. One of the reasons is because he practices self-control. He is fair, generous, patient, and controls his emotions. Josh wants to be like his brother, so he watches and learns from him.

When you were small, you wanted to be like your parents. Watch a small child try to do what Mom or Dad is doing. Whom do you admire in your family? Do you try to practice the same behavior?

If you are an older brother or sister, keep in mind that the young ones will learn from you. What do you want them to imitate, your good behavior or your poor behavior?

We have seen how self-control is innate yet is also learned from interaction with our family. Society also sets standards for our behavior. Within a society are many institutions such as school, government, religious organizations, and so on. All

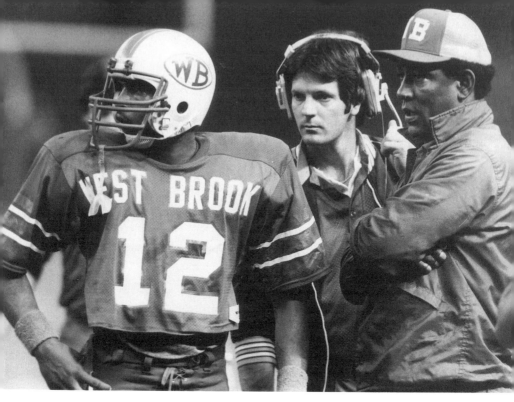

Once you are working toward a goal, self-control is easier.

follow basically the same values; however, each institution has some special rules.

For example, there are ways to behave at school. You must study and respect your elders. The same rules apply in church or synagogue. They also apply to government, although you may not get homework assignments from traffic court.

You have to wait your turn to speak in history class and at a city council meeting, but you might be required to speak out in church or P.E. class.

Because of the differences, there are many sets of behavior to learn. If you live in a complex society or are involved in many activities, it becomes even more involved.

The best help in learning self-control in society is to decide what is important to you. Look at the environments you are involved with: football team, choir, band, country club. List them in order of importance to you.

When your list is made, decide on the goals you want to achieve within each environment. If you want to be the star quarterback in your senior year or a pro football player, you have to set different controls on your life.

Having goals helps you to control your actions. If you are a musician you won't act without thinking when you're changing a tire on a cold day. You will control your anger and annoyance and handle the tools carefully so as not to hurt your hands.

If you're on the gymnastics team and there is a match tomorrow, you will control your drinking at the party if you have a goal to win the match.

A person who respects and practices religious values and morals will find it easier to control moderation, anger, and malicious gossip.

Look at what you admire and enjoy, then set your goals. After that you can focus your control so that it will help you accomplish those goals. It's like a reward.

Society teaches you to operate on a reward system. There is a reward or a consequence for everything you do. By setting your goals, *you* decide how rewarding your life will be.

Let's look at Kenneth and Martha and see how their goals help them maintain self-control.

Martha grabbed the plastic cooler from the dock and set it in the speedboat. The craft tilted as she leaned forward, but Martha easily balanced against the rocking movement. Since she had been water-skiing with Kenneth these past weeks, she had become a pro at handling the boat's rocking motion.

"All set?" Kenneth asked as he tossed the mooring ropes into the bow.

Martha glanced up and had to pause to admire how the sunlight glistened on his tanned skin. Kenneth was not only terrific looking, but he was a wonderful person. She smiled, thankful that she had been lucky enough to meet him.

When he caught her staring, he put his fists on his hips. "Loafing on the job again?" he accused.

"No." She smiled. "Just admiring the scenery."

He tried to pretend it didn't matter, but she could tell he enjoyed her flattery.

"It's not bad from here, either," he told her.

Embarrassed now, she started putting their gear in the pouches and cabinets. "You'd better hop in. If we don't get going, we'll never get any skiing done."

"Now you want to hurry," he teased.

He wasn't really objecting. The wind always came up after noon and made the water too choppy to ski. If they wanted to enjoy the sport, they had to take off soon.

Kenneth backed the boat away from the dock. Martha couldn't help feeling proud as they cruised past the clubhouse. She and Kenneth made a fine-looking couple; everyone said so.

The morning passed quickly as they skied in their favorite cove. By lunch time, Martha's muscles ached and she was starving.

"Where shall we eat?" she asked. "Are we going to the cove?"

The sandy beach at the cove was where all their friends gathered. The only way to get there was by boat. Since it wasn't supervised, the partying got pretty wild at times. Even though Martha didn't always join in, she enjoyed watching and visiting with her friends.

Kenneth surprised her today though. "Let's not go there. I have a special place in mind."

"Oh?" Her curiosity was aroused. He sounded so mysterious. "Are we going back to the clubhouse?"

"Nope." He smiled.

"Good. It's too crowded there."

"Exactly. That's what I want. Privacy."

"I like that." Martha smiled back as excitement traced through her. She had no objection to being alone with Kenneth.

The place Kenneth took her to did surprise her. When he said alone, he meant it. The inlet wound into the tree-lined shore. When Kenneth anchored the boat they were surrounded by underbrush, trees, and granite. The lake was totally out of sight.

"Let's stay here." Kenneth patted the cushions of the boat. "It's more comfortable."

Martha eyed the scratchy underbrush and her bare legs. "You're right. I'm game for a picnic in the boat."

Kenneth helped her set out the food. Conversation stayed light as they ate. Kenneth always had a wealth of funny stories. He told her his newest ones.

"I love the way you laugh," she told him.

Suddenly he grew serious. He set his can of soda down and scooted close to her. "Do you?"

She nodded, her heart suddenly beating faster.

"What else do you love about me?" He put his arm across her shoulder.

Martha set down her soda also. She turned slightly to look into his eyes. "Probably about everything."

Her answer must have pleased him, because the next thing she knew he was kissing her. Martha slipped her arms around his neck and pulled him closer. Being like this with Kenneth was heaven.

For endless minutes they stayed close together. Passion built as they traced the skin left bare by bikini swimsuits. Martha easily forgot about the real world. Right now there was only the two of them. They were all that mattered.

An engine roared past and intruded on their intimacy. Kenneth pulled away to check that they were still alone. Martha tried to catch her breath. Her heart was pounding. She wanted Kenneth to make love to her.

To her dismay, he didn't return to her side. She brushed back her tousled hair and tried to see what he was doing. His position alarmed her. He sat with his elbows braced on his knees, his head held between his hands.

"I'm sorry, Martha," he whispered.

"Sorry for what?" She moved closer to him, but he backed away. Her stomach clenched with apprehension. What was the matter?

"I love you," he said. "I want to make love to you, but we can't."

The truth of his words made her joyful and sad. "Of course, we can't. You have years of school ahead of you."

"And you?" He turned to face her. "What do you plan to do after graduation? Don't you still want to become a teacher?"

She nodded as the thought of their future yawned endlessly before them. Five years for a teaching certificate. He had more than that for training as a doctor.

"We both have plans. We can't blow them by messing around now."

Martha took a deep breath as she fought the frustration mingled with relief. "I know you're right. I shouldn't have let it get this far."

Quickly he slid close and grabbed her hand. "Don't be sorry we kissed. At least we have that."

"But it's not enough."

His fingers tightened around hers. "I know. It will never be enough." He paused for a moment and then continued, his voice shaky with nerves. "I want to ask you to marry me, but we're too young."

Her heart raced. "Marry?"

"Would you?" His expression was pleading, yet frightened too.

Martha understood. She was terrified, but at the same time she wanted to jump on the bow of the boat and shout.

"I love you, Kenneth Rawlins. Of course I'll marry you."

"But what about school and our plans for the future?"

"That's it," Martha said. "The future. We'll wait at least until I'm done with school. Then we'll marry. I can teach while you do your internship."

"But that's five years away."

"I've heard of longer engagements."

Kenneth ran his fingers through his hair. "Man, I don't know if this will work."

"Sure it will, because we care and we know what we want. We'll manage," Martha promised.

For the rest of the afternoon they discussed plans for the future. It was going to be a long wait, but Martha had no doubt that they would do it. They were both determined.

What self-control did Kenneth and Martha show? Kenneth wanted to speak to Martha so he exerted control by finding a private place to talk instead of crowding around their peers.

Both Kenneth and Martha wanted sex, but they controlled their urge. Do you understand why? Can you see how their goals helped them strengthen their convictions?

If you want something enough, you can exert all kinds of self-control to get it. An athlete will practice moderation and resist any substance that will harm his or her body. A person who wants to be a police officer will make every effort to be moral, honest, and fair.

People who want to work in public service need to control their manners and patience. Malicious gossip, anger, and obscene language will not be tolerated in public positions. Can you imagine the mayor of your city being elected if he or she didn't have those emotions under control?

What kind of husband or wife will you be if jealousy is not controlled? What kind of friend are you if you let envy rule your life?

Think about what you want to be. How do you want society to view you? You make the decision on how close to your ideal you get by how you choose to act. By practicing self-control, you come closer to your ideal. By letting the control slide, you move farther away from the image you want.

In review, the way to develop self-control is: (1) to learn to listen to your sixth sense, which is your innate monitor for self-control; (2) to look at those around you whom you admire, study their behavior, and observe how they maintain self-control; and (3) to set goals for yourself and chart the course needed to accomplish them. Having well-defined goals gives you the strength to practice self-control.

Remember also that making changes in your life to improve your self-control can be done, but it is a slow process. Don't be discouraged if you don't see immediate results. Your brain is like a computer: it needs to be reprocessed. Take out the bad and self-destructive habits. Put in the new constructive patterns of morality, honesty, fairness, and manners. Control the negative emotions of malicious gossip, obscene language, anger, jealousy, and envy.

Finally, expand your ability to perceive your sixth sense. Work on becoming moderate, generous, forgiving, patient, and compassionate. Those are the elements of self-control that will provide you with the best possible quality of life.

CHAPTER 6

Why Self-control Is Important

The measure of self-control exerted by a person, an organization, or a society shows others who and what they are. Self-control is observable. You can see how much composure a person has. A controlled society reflects discipline and moderation. The harmony is evident.

It is important to understand this universal law. Self-control is valued in every culture and society. If you want to be perceived as a valuable person, organization, or society, you must decide to show moderation and morality. You must be fair, honest, and forgiving. Emotions such as anger, jealousy, and envy must be curbed. You must not gossip. You must treat others with compassion, generosity, and patience.

How well you manage to do these things states what type of person, organization, or society you are.

WHAT SELF-CONTROL SAYS ABOUT AN INDIVIDUAL

Remember the definition of self-control from Chapter 1? It is *the power to direct or regulate a person's identity, character, or personal interest.* By directing your identity, character, and interest, you define who you are.

Look at all the elements of self-control and test yourself against them. How honest, fair, and moderate are you? Are these qualities that you want to be known for? If so, you need to *be* honest, fair, and moderate.

How well do you control your anger? Do you use obscene language and pass on malicious gossip? If you exhibit these elements, how do people perceive you? Will they want to be around you?

Do you like to be with compassionate, generous, and patient people? Would you like others to consider you in that way? Think about what you need to do for that to happen.

How other people perceive you depends on how you act. It has very little to do with them. It has everything to do with *you.* Each person determines his or her own degree of self-control. It is up to you to decide how you want the world to know you.

Let's look at four friends and see how they decide who they are.

Robyn hurried down the hall toward Room 103 where the Journalism Club was meeting. She was going to be late again. It wasn't her fault she had run into Mr. Brown and stopped to talk to him about the basketball team's prospects for the game tonight.

Quickly she slipped into the room and tried to sit down quietly. It didn't work.

Wayne swung around and glared. "Late again, Robyn."

"Don't bug me," she quickly countered. "I was getting facts for the sports page."

"Likely story. You always have some excuse, but the real fact of the matter is, you're always late."

Robyn made a face at him before settling her notebook on the desk. "Quit complaining, Wayne. You're just jealous because I always get the best stories."

"Ha. That's a laugh. I'll have you know that the principal thought my piece on the test frauds was ..."

"Enough!" Miguel pounded his fist on the table. "Susanna and I want to get this meeting over with. We have work to do."

Wayne looked angry. His face was mottled. Robyn laughed.

Before Wayne could explode, Miguel spoke. "Susanna will go over our assignments, and then we can end this meeting."

Susanna smiled and looked at Robyn, then Wayne. Robyn relaxed. Susanna was never a threat. In fact, Robyn always felt calm around the dark-haired girl. She liked Susanna's easy-going manner. She wished she had that kind of patience.

"There are rumors that the English department is going to require another literature course for graduation."

"What?" Wayne jumped up.

Robyn felt like doing the same. She pounded her fist on her desktop and swore.

Susanna stared at both of them until they quieted down. "It won't help matters to swear about it. Nor can we write anything until we've investigated the situation."

"That's what you think!" Wayne began to pace. "This will make a great headline. Can you picture how riled everyone will get?"

Miguel tapped his pencil on his notebook. "I'm taking this story, Wayne, and we'll wait until we have all the facts before we publish it."

Robyn watched the interplay between Wayne and Miguel. Wayne should have realized that Miguel would not let him sensationalize the story. Miguel was too honest for that.

When they had quieted down, Robyn dropped her bombshell. "I've got a lead story, and it's backed up with facts."

Everyone turned to look at her. Robyn took her time, enjoying her moment of glory.

"Well," Susanna said, "are you going to tell us or will it be a surprise?"

"You're going to be surprised all right." Robyn couldn't help the smirk creasing her face.

Miguel must have been made suspicious by her expression, because suddenly he was wary. "What kind of story do you have, Robyn? We aren't printing smut like your story on Miss Greene's sex life."

They had missed a good opportunity there, all right. Exposing an affair between two single teachers was hot news. Robyn crossed her arms defensively. "This isn't smut, but it is a scandal." She gloated. "Mr. Davis was arrested last night for possession of drugs."

"The science teacher?"

"None other." Robyn sat back, enjoying the expressions of horror and disgust crossing their faces.

"How did you hear about that?" Miguel wanted to know.

"Don't you trust me?" Robyn asked, annoyed by the question.

"Well, you aren't exactly known for your ethics," Miguel told her.

Robyn sat back, clamping her jaw tight. She wouldn't give Miguel the satisfaction of knowing that his comment had hurt.

Susanna spoke up. "Let's not start in on each other. We'll never get anything accomplished that way."

Good old Susanna, Robyn thought. Always the one to keep the peace.

"I have reliable sources, and I want to print it."

Susanna frowned. "I don't know. Do we really want to cast our teachers in such a negative light?"

"*We* aren't making him look bad," Wayne said. "He was the one doing drugs. He did it to himself."

"True, but we don't need to make it worse by sensation-alizing the scandal."

Wayne groaned. "Come off it, Susanna. That's what news is all about."

Susanna straightened in her seat. Robyn watched with admiration. Susanna was soft-hearted, but she stood by her ideals. She wasn't a pushover. Wayne would find out the hard way if he tangled with her.

Susanna's voice was low and determined. "The man is innocent until a court proves him guilty. If we print anything at all, it will be that he was charged with possession of drugs."

Tension crackled throughout the room, but Susanna held her ground. Miguel supported her. Wayne wanted a big story, as did Robyn. She could feel anger building within her. It wasn't fair. Susanna always got her way.

With the exception of Wayne's outburst, most of the instances of self-control and lack of it were subtle. Were you able to determine all the various shades?

Who showed honesty, fairness, and moderation? Who was patient, generous, and compassionate? Did anyone lose control with malice, anger, obscene language, envy, or jealousy? When and how?

Can you describe each person's character from his or her behavior? By their speech and actions, you know who was in control and who wasn't. You know what type of person each of the four is. Which one would you want to be like?

By identifying people's character from their behavior, you learn whether you can trust them or not. You can tell if they are someone you want to associate with. Which student from the Journalism Club would you want writing a story about you? Why?

Another characteristic we notice about people from their self-control is how responsible they are. Which of the four students acted responsibly? Can you think of instances when you practiced self-control and it showed others how responsible you were?

If you are honest, you can be trusted to work on a job where you handle money. If you are fair, patient, and serene, you can work with other people. Your control of your emotions proves to people that you are a responsible person.

A self-controlled person is also considered reliable. If you can practice moderation and say no to alcohol and other drugs, your parents will probably allow you to go to parties and be involved in events at school.

If you have proved unreliable because you didn't practice self-control, you will be barred from many activities. A person who drinks too much and becomes violent is not invited to parties. People who get angry on the highway and vent that anger with reckless driving lose their driver's license. People who gossip maliciously soon lose friends.

Your control measures how conservative you are. Some people are flamboyant and show off all the time. Some people are shy and withdrawn, others are loud and boisterous. The point is that everyone is different. They all have their own levels of self-control.

The wonderful thing for you to understand is that you can be who *you* want to be. All you have to do is regulate your self-control. Set goals, watch those you admire, and listen to your instincts. You can become who you want to be. The choice is yours.

Two brothers, Nathan and Jordan, illustrate how that works.

Nathan staggered slightly as he made his way up the driveway. He shouldn't have had that last drink. At least Barbara had brought him home from the party.

The cement seemed to buckle as he tried to walk. He leaned against the car parked in front of the garage and glanced at his watch. The light flickered when he clicked the digital on. It took a second to focus, but he finally saw that it was twelve-thirty.

Good, he thought. The folks couldn't get bent out of shape about the hour. He stumbled and fell. Several of his favorite profanities burst from his mouth.

Suddenly the porch light flicked on. "What's all that racket? Is that you, Nathan?"

Nathan swore again as he gripped the door handle of the car. "Pipe down. You want to call out the whole neighborhood?"

His younger brother, Jordan, came into view. Nathan reached for him. "Where's Mom and Dad? I don't want you calling them out here."

Jordan swung Nathan's arm across his shoulders. "Whew! You smell like a brewery. You been at a party again?"

"Yep." Nathan tried to straighten. He wanted to be cool for his little brother. "Went with Barbara. It was at Eddie's house."

"Why'd you go with Barbara?" Jordan let go of Nathan but watched every move he made. "I thought you didn't like her."

"Why d'you think?" Nathan wiggled his brows and leered.

Jordan groaned. "She's been out with every guy at school. I hope you had some protection on you."

"No sweat," Nathan said, but inwardly he swore again. He hadn't bought any goods at the drugstore. He shouldn't have screwed around, but he had been so blasted and so turned on.

"Come on." Jordan reached for Nathan. "We'd better get you to bed before Mom and Dad catch sight of you."

Nathan backed up. "Don't touch me. I can walk by myself."

At least he had thought he could. Suddenly he was flying through the air. It was weird. He crashed into the car and leaned across the hood. It was so funny. He laughed until the hiccups started.

"Nathan, be careful." Jordan sounded strained.

"Calm down, little bro. I've got everything under control."

"You're messing up my car."

Nathan was starting to rise when what Jordan had said sank in. Carefully he pulled himself upright, although he continued to lean on the fender.

"*Your* car?" Nathan asked.

Jordan's expression brightened. "Yeah. it's my birthday today."

Nathan let out another stream of profanities. He had forgotten the kid's birthday. His folks would be angry.

"Sorry, kid. I got you something, though. It's upstairs."

He could give him his new album. He had only listened to it once. But what the heck, Jordan wouldn't know the difference.

"That's all right. I understand." Jordan patted him on the shoulder.

Nathan forced himself not to reject the gesture. It was the least he could do since he had missed the family celebration. Still . . .

"Why don't you get mad or something?" he asked Jordan. "Don't you know your attitude makes me sick? Always so lily pure."

Jordan backed up as if he had been slapped. "It's no good talking to you when you're like this. Why don't we go in?"

Nathan backed away but lost his balance again and fell on top of the car.

"Hey!" Jordan grabbed his hand and yanked him off. "My car."

"Yeah, right. Since when do you have a car like this?"

"Today. Mom and Dad gave it to me for my birthday. I'm sixteen, remember?"

Nathan shook his head, sure he hadn't heard right. Jordan couldn't possibly receive a car for his birthday. If anyone were to get a car it would be Nathan. After all, he was the oldest.

"Come off it. I'm in no shape to kid around. Whose car is it?"

"Mine. I swear it's the truth." Jordan held up his fingers in the symbol they used as kids.

"I don't believe it."

"If you had been here for the party you would have known. We all went for a ride in it already."

Red-hot anger suddenly erupted in Nathan. He jerked away from Jordan and ran up the walk to the front door. With no attempt to be quiet or careful, he charged in while the door slammed against the wall.

"*Mother!*" He shouted. His voice echoed in the house.

Footsteps hurried toward him. His mother came running out of the living room until she caught sight of Nathan. Out of his side vision he saw Jordan beside him.

"What's going on?" Nathan yelled. "Don't tell me you and Dad bought Jordan a car?"

His mother looked pale, but he didn't care. He couldn't believe what was happening. Suddenly his father loomed behind his mother. Nathan paused for a second until he thought of the shiny red sports car parked out front.

"I want to know why Jordan has a car." His voice sounded like a growl. Tough. He felt like growling and snarling and tearing his brother to bits.

"You don't talk to your mother like that," his father said in a stern voice.

"Come in and sit down, Son. We'll talk this out."

Nathan wanted to scream, but he knew his parents would simply retreat into the living room. He had to follow, but he spoke every foul word he could think of while doing so.

His father swung around. "What have we told you about swearing in this house?"

Nathan could have argued, but he refrained. He wanted some answers.

"Why does Jordan have a car?"

"He turned sixteen," his mother stated calmly.

Dad elaborated. "He has worked hard to earn money for the insurance, his grades are up, and he's responsible. We trusted him to own his own car."

The words were like a slap in the face. To make it worse, Nathan had the feeling they had been rehearsed before he got home.

"You always do everything for Jordan. What about me? I didn't get a car when I turned sixteen. I still have to bum rides from my friends."

"And we pray they haven't been drinking like you," Mom said.

"Right." Nathan swore again in spite of his father's anger. "Use that as an excuse."

"It isn't an excuse, but the truth."

"What's wrong with my drinking? You always have a drink before dinner."

"One, Son. We have only one. There's a difference between enjoying a cocktail and getting drunk."

Nathan started to argue, but when his father lifted his hand for silence Nathan shut up. He knew better than to go too far.

"Enough of this discussion. We've had it many times before. You know our feelings on the matter, and you know we don't approve of your behavior."

"You never do," Nathan raged. "It's always Jordan this and Jordan that. How come he gets all the favors? All I ever get is flak."

Tears trickled down his mother's cheeks. For a second he felt remorse, but it didn't last long. Jordan was shifting from one foot to the other, obviously feeling guilty. He should, too.

"It's not fair. I should have the car, not Jordan."

His father heaved a sigh as if he were very tired. "You can have a car when you prove that we can trust you."

"Trust? Of course, you can trust me. Do you think I'd run off and sell the thing or something?"

"It's not that, and you know it." His father's temper was rising now. "You drink too much. You never study, and where were you tonight? You're not responsible, Son."

"Son?" Nathan couldn't stand another minute. "Son? How can you call me son when you don't treat me like one?"

Before his father could respond, Nathan charged out the door. He'd show them he didn't need them or their favoritism. If they thought Jordan was so hot, they could have him all to themselves. He was going to split.

Nathan did not perceive his family as being fair, generous, or caring. What do you think? Why wouldn't they give Nathan his own car? Would you if you were his parents?

Nathan felt that he was being treated unfairly. Whose fault was that? Often we think others are treating us badly and we don't have any control over the matter.

Nathan did not see that his behavior determined how his

parents saw and treated him. He felt that they were being unfair. Jordan was getting better treatment.

In reality, Nathan is the one who controlled how his parents reacted to him. His parents did not make him drink. His parents did not keep him from studying. His parents did not force him to use obscene language.

Nathan himself determined those things. He is the one who swore, drank, and fooled around. No one forced him to. He decided of his own free will.

If that is the case, why do you think he is so surprised at how he is treated? Jordan has the same parents, the same house and advantages that Nathan does. Yet Jordan chose a different path to follow. Jordan practices self-control and conforms to the rules of his family. He studies, does not party all the time, and uses manners with his parents. He doesn't indulge in dangerous sexual practices either.

Can you see how the brothers are perceived differently and why? Both brothers were judged by their behavior. They decided their own behavior. What they do shows the world their true character.

Your mastery of self determines who you are. No one else can set out rules. They can influence you. However, the ultimate choice remains with you. That is why it is important for a person to maintain self-control.

WHAT SELF-CONTROL SAYS ABOUT A SOCIETY

Just as persons are judged by their self-control, so is a society. Cultural values are mirrored in the actions of the members of each group. This happens in the same way as with an individual. It occurs within organizations and institutions. Communities and countries are also judged by their measure of self-control.

Just as you are known by your actions, you are also identified with your associates. The social groups in existence today are reflections of the self-control their members practice.

Think about organizations around you. Try to define them by

Other people see you in terms of the company you keep.

the elements of self-control. Are they known for their honesty, morals, fairness, or moderation? Do they exhibit uncontrolled anger, obscene language, envy, or jealousy? Do they gossip with malice or mean intent? Can you see patience, compassion, and generosity within the system?

These elements define an organization, a community, and a country in the same way they define you. Because the organization, community, or country can be defined, its members are given the same definition.

For example, think of a street gang. What elements of control do they exhibit? They aren't known for control of anger, malice, or obscene language. But what if Craig belongs to the street gang and doesn't lose his temper, never swears, and is generous and kind.

How is Craig considered by those around him? Perhaps his family and friends who know him well believe that he is self-controlled, but does the general public? Most of society will judge Craig by the reputation of the gang.

That may not sound fair, but it is the reality. If Craig wants to be known in his true light, he has two options. He can leave the gang and assume his own identity, or he can take steps to change the image of the gang.

It will be easier for Craig to leave the gang and identify with others more like himself. That is not always possible, however. He may need to remain in the gang for protection from neighboring gangs.

Some situations may seem impossible to escape or to change, but if you practice self-control you will find a way.

Dr. Martin Luther King was given characteristics associated with his race. A false image of black Americans existed. He couldn't very well escape the identity, as it was impossible to change the color of his skin. What he did was to change the image of his society. He demanded that black Americans be considered equal to white Americans, and he tried to organize and educate the members of the society both black and white to exhibit self-control and make the change.

Not all of the organizations we associate with are negative. We can sometimes look better than we really are by associating with a community that has high ideals and self-control.

An example might be a religious organization. It may be known for its compassion, generosity, and forgiving nature. It may be considered fair, honest, and moderate. On the whole, its members probably practice self-control with regard to emotional displays of anger, malice, jealousy, obscene language, and envy.

You probably know people, though, who belong to such an organization but are not self-controlled. Some gossip. Others are jealous, and still others use obscene language.

The fact that you belong to this organization does not give you the control the organization is known for. Belonging to it probably influences you to practice self-control, but it cannot force you to do so. Again it is *you* who decides your actions.

The organization and your association with it will be judged by the action of its leaders and majority. That is also true of a community or a country.

Let's consider how this works in communities. Small simple communities seem to have a more controlled population; the organizations are few, the life is simple, and roles are well defined. Because everyone knows what the other person is doing, it is easier to exert societal pressure.

In small communities, everyone has a well-defined role and knows what behavior others expect.

If you grow up in a small community you either learn to conform or you rebel. By practicing self-control, you can fit into the cultural morals and laws of the community. If you don't practice self-control you are considered a misfit and may be cast out.

That is a strong incentive for self-control but is still no guarantee. It is within the person's power to practice control or not. You decide if you want to be part of the community.

In a large community, such as a metropolitan area, the rules are not as clear nor as defined. That gives you freedom through anonymity, but it also gives you more opportunity to be lax on using self-control.

Lack of self-control leads to destruction. You can see evidence of that in large cities where gangs control the streets.

Prostitution, drugs, pornography, and crime abound. It isn't that people are less moral in large communities. It is simply a case of not seeing the need to practice self-control.

Eventually this behavior will destroy the individual. Cities that have not dealt with their problems nor attempted to solve them are also dying. Everyone likes the idea of having the freedom to do as they please, but using that freedom irresponsibly leads to destruction.

History has proved this time and time again. Study the rise and fall of urban areas. In your studies you will see, though, that destructive patterns can be changed. It involves one important element, and that is self-control.

Communities need to practice nonviolence, patience, perseverance, and many other traits of control. They need to establish clear-cut rules and enforce them. That gives members the incentive to follow them or suffer the consequences.

Nations are also judged by their display of self-control. Think of countries in the world today and list the elements of control they are known for. If you meet someone from that country how will you react at first? You will probably assume that he or she represents the stereotype of citizens of that country. When you get to know the person you will probably discover otherwise.

For example, many foreigners are afraid to come to the United States. They see on the television news the reports of crime in the streets, drugs, gangs, and riots, and they think all of America is like that.

When Americans visit those people, they either prove that the concept is true or show that it is false. Each one of you acts as an ambassador of whatever country, community, or organization you belong to. If you want the world to view your group, city, and country with respect, you need to control your behavior so that respect will be developed.

You may think that you as an individual cannot shape world opinions of your culture, but in fact you can. Every act of kindness brings that element into focus. Every show of compassion generates good feelings around you.

Avoiding obscene language and curbing anger brings peace and harmony. Showing moderation and manners instead of envy and jealousy strengthens the moral fiber of your environment.

Morality

Think of the groups or organizations that are most important to you. List the moral values they are known for. How many of those values do you practice?

For example, if you and your friends belong to a religious organization, how well do you control your behavior so that you practice the morals of that organization? Is the organization considered generous? Are you?

If moral laws exist that you should not steal or swear, you represent your organization by not stealing or swearing. If you do swear, for example, and other people hear you, they will think that your organization must not be very strong or controlled.

You represent the community you live in. If foreigners land in New York and their luggage is promptly stolen, their fears about the United States are confirmed. If on the other hand a person is helpful and kind in helping them find a hotel, that person represents Americans as patient and generous.

Honesty

Honesty is a reflection of your society. Every culture has laws that require its members to be honest. Some cultures are known for their honesty. The Amish in Pennsylvania and the islanders of Tristan da Cunha share a reputation for open communities in which theft and dishonesty do not occur. What had to happen to make the world believe that? Each person in those communities practices self-control and *is* honest. By each individual's effort, the whole culture is credited with honesty.

The Amish have a widespread reputation for being honest, hardworking people.

Look at your community. How much honesty is practiced in it? If you and the majority of the people use self-control and exhibit honest behavior, your community is probably viewed as honest.

Unfortunately, large countries such as the United States are not viewed that way. Too many individuals are dishonest in their pursuit of personal gain to make other countries believe they can be trusted.

Fairness

In democratic countries where laws and court systems are designed to ensure fair and equal treatment, it is reasonable to consider the societies fair. Again, it is individuals and groups within the society that make a lie out of the claim.

Some corporations use money and power to buy their way out of justice. When that happens it reflects on the society that lets it happen. If, however, most of the people obey the laws and suffer consequences when they don't, that society will be considered fair.

Some societies operate under dictatorships where the selfish interests of one person or political group are the only ones considered. Those societies are generally viewed as unfair by the standards of democratic countries. This judgment is relative and can only be decided on the basis of the society you belong to.

Again, it is the individuals who determine how the culture is viewed. If most of its members are fair, the community is considered just.

Manners

Manners reflect the self-control of a society, but like fairness, they can be judged only by those within the culture. What are good manners in your culture may be poor manners in another country.

The organizations and subcultures within your society, however, reflect their control by the standard of manners they observe. A group of Boy Scouts reflect a high standard of morality and practice good manners. That group is considered polite as long as its members use self-control and are polite.

You may have heard the term the "ugly American." Some people believe Americans have bad manners because when they travel to another country they don't bother to learn and practice the manners of that culture. This impolite behavior reflects on American society as a whole. Each person needs to make an effort to be polite when in a foreign country.

Malicious Gossip

Eveyone knows people who spoil a social club or a committee at school by gossiping. Unfortunately this happens often, but you can keep it from ruining the group by changing the subject or saying something positive each time it occurs. Remember that each person contributes to the image of the group. If you refuse to allow gossip around you, it will disappear — at least in your presence. If others follow your example, you will change the negativity of the group and save it from destroying itself with malice. The group will have a positive image and be known for its pleasant company.

Obscene Language

Language defines a culture. It expresses the thinking and values by its words and ideas. A group or a society that uses obscene language projects other lacks of self-control such as anger, poor manners, unforgiveness, and lack of compassion.

Obscene language insults, offends, and incites to poor behavior. Sometimes it is appropriate, but on the whole it represents negative elements. If you use obscene language or associate with others who do, you are projecting an image of poor self-control.

Imagine you are in a shopping mall and you suddenly hear a conversation of obscene language. What is your immediate reaction? You may become defensive. Perhaps you will be fearful because you associate the language with mean and dangerous people.

Remember, you are an ambassador of your family and society. You are judged by the language you use. Think about how you want others to view you, and use the appropriate language for that image.

Anger

Latin Americans are culturally known for fiery tempers, but it is a stereotype that does not apply to every Latin American. Believing that every Latin American is angry is an unfair judgment, yet the stereotype exists because many members of that group express public anger.

White supremacist groups show extreme anger and hate. They are known as angry groups because when they are together they show angry and mean behavior.

The Black Panthers during the civil rights movement were known for anger and violence. Its members were considered by the majority of society as basically uncontrolled.

What behavior defines these subcultures as angry? Do they practice self-control in dealing with others? When you associate with an angry culture, you will be identified in those terms. Remember that lack of self-control leads to destruction. Study the history of these *angry* groups and find out what did happen to them.

Jealousy

A jealous person is one most people want to stay away from. Irrational behavior and lack of self-control make him or her dangerous and unpleasant to be around.

The same caution exists around a jealous organization or society. Remember that the definition of jealousy is the desire for something that someone else has. If an organization or community or even a country has a strong enough desire and the power to back it up, it can be a real threat.

Wars have started because a jealous nation wanted the

Members of the Ku Klux Klan incite people to acts of racial hatred.

wealth and power of another. Organizations have become mobs when trying to gain something that wasn't theirs. Consider carefully the dangers of jealous behavior, individually or collectively.

Envy

Along with jealousy, envy has played a major role in history. The Spanish envied the Aztecs and Incas their gold. The French peasants envied the French royalty their wealth and power. The Russian Communists envied the Russian aristocracy their rights. All of these instances of envy led to war and destruction. Nations war against nations for power and resources.

The same thing happens when communities and organizations do not control their envy. Instead of building on what they have, they destroy the environment or each other to gain what they envy. Gangs steal and deal drugs because they want wealth.

What can happen to you if you let envy control your life? Controlling envy can lead to a healthier environment. Each person must do his or her share of control for it to affect the whole.

Moderation

Extreme behavior always attracts attention. If a society is too strict or too lax, there are conflicting consequences. The control most cultures strive for is moderation. If the society has strong elements of self-control it can enjoy the peace and harmony of moderation.

Think about your own behavior. When do things run the smoothest, when you are really excited and up, or when you are totally depressed and down? They probably operate best when you are feeling a steady moderation.

The extremes cause reactions that are too fast and sudden, which lead to mistakes. Remember the sixth sense? It applies to societies as well. Move at a moderate pace and consider all angles before you take each step.

Forgiveness

Groups of people who seek revenge are frightening. A vengeful society is dangerous. Organizations that cannot forgive display behavior that is uncontrolled and judgmental.

Religious organizations, community services, and mental health clinics offer forgiveness. They do not judge but suggest solutions to the problems to be faced.

Individuals strengthen the image of their culture by forgiving others. Release from guilt strengthens a society. That strength can be used to change unwanted behavior.

Blame, accusations, and judgments weaken a society by heaping guilt and shame. What kind of society do you want to be part of — a forgiving or a vengeful nation? You need to exert your measure of control to make it happen.

Generosity

Few people stop to realize this aspect of the United States, but one of the reasons it is such a powerful country is that it is basically a generous nation. How many countries receive aid from the U.S.? How many countries have survived because of American generosity?

After World War II the United States helped its former enemies. How did that ultimately benefit the U.S.?

Internally the United States practices generosity: free education, welfare programs for the poor, special services for the sick. Generosity breeds healthy prosperity.

Consider the alternatives, and you will see the need for a society as well as an individual to remain generous.

Patience

A patient organization or country is a tolerant society. It practices reasonable laws and takes measures to enforce them. A patient society is a joy to live in. Everyone makes mistakes. It

Under Stalin's rule, people in the Soviet Union lived with fear and suspicion. For many years his likeness was displayed in a tailor's window in Budapest, Hungary.

is reassuring to know that a degree of leniency allows for mistakes and growth.

Some countries are extreme and intolerant. In the early days of the Soviet Union people could not even express opinions without severe penalties. Living in such an environment is stressful and oppressive.

To guarantee that your society practices patience, everyone needs to control their own indulgences and practice a tolerant attitude. If you are patient with others, you will encourage them to be more accepting also.

Compassion

There are organizations or groups or individuals in any society that people always turn to when in need because they portray the image of compassion and practice a loving nature.

Compassion is mirrored in a society just as it shines from a person. Compassion draws positive responses and behavior. It brings good to those who share it. A strong society is one known for its caring and sharing, for its gracious, humane goodness.

Self-control is valued. Individuals must practice it to survive. Organizations, communities, and nations reflect the self-control practiced by their members and citizens.

By maintaining your own self-control, you contribute to the well-being of your society. Cultures are defined by their members. You make the difference as to whether your society is controlled or not. Your behavior determines the quality of your life. It is in *your* control.

Bibliography

Nonfiction

Adler, David A. *Martin Luther King, Jr. — Free at Last*. New York: Holiday House, 1986.

Boyer, Ruth G. *The Happy Adolescent*. Palo Alto, CA: R & E Research Associates, 1981.

Buckalew, M. W., Jr. *Learning to Control Stress*. Rosen Publishing Group, 1979.

Cohen, Susan and Daniel. *Teenage Stress*. New York: M. Evans & Company, 1972.

Collier, James Lincoln. *The Hard Life of the Teenager*. New York: Four Winds Press, 1972.

Davidson, Margaret. *I Have a Dream*. New York: Scholastic, Inc., 1986.

Gawain, Shakti. *Creative Visualization*. Mill Valley, CA: Whatever Publishing, 1978.

Kreskin. *Kreskin's Mind Power Book*. New York: McGraw-Hill Book Company, 1977.

London, Kathleen. *Who Am I? Who Are You?* Reading, MA: Addison-Wesley Publishing Co., 1983.

Moolman, Valerie. *How to Get Along with Yourself*. New York: Castle Books, 1969.

Newman, Mildred, and Berkowitz, Bernard. *How to Take Charge of Your Life*. New York: Bantam Books, 1978.

Schwarzrock, Shirley. *Do I Know the "Me" Others See?* Circle Pines, MN: American Guidance Service, 1973.

Verdal, Joyce L. *I Dare You*. New York: Holt, Rinehart & Winston, 1983.

Fiction

Conford, Ellen. *The Things I Did for Love*. New York: Bantam Books, 1987.

Cooney, Caroline B. *Among Friends*. New York: Bantam Books, 1987.

Cooney, Linda A. *Class of '89, Senior*. New York: Scholastic, Inc., 1988.

Corbin, William. *A Dog Worth Stealing*. New York: Orchard Books, 1987.

Guy, Rosa. *And I Heard a Bird Sing*. New York: Delacorte Press, 1987.

Hayes, Sheila. *No Autographs, Please*. New York: Lodestar Books, E. P. Dutton, 1984.

Oppenheim, Joan L. *A Clown Like Me*. New York: Thomas Y. Crowell, 1985.

Pfeffer, Susan Beth. *Fantasy Summer*. New York: Pacer Books, 1984.

White, Ellen Emerson. *Life Without Friends*. New York: Scholastic, Inc., 1987.

Index